NATIONAL ACADEMIES *Sciences Engineering Medicine*

NATIONAL ACADEMIES PRESS
Washington, DC

National Science, Technology, and Security Roundtable Capstone

Karla Hagan, *Rapporteur*

National Science, Technology, and Security Roundtable

Policy and Global Affairs

Proceedings of a Workshop

NATIONAL ACADEMIES PRESS 500 Fifth Street, NW Washington, DC 20001

This activity was supported by the United States Department of Defense under award numbers W911NF18D0002 and W911NF20F0052, the National Institutes of Health under award HHSN2632018000291/75N98020F00015, and the National Science Foundation under award number 2154341. Any opinions, findings, conclusions, or recommendations expressed in this publication do not necessarily reflect the views of any organization or agency that provided support for the roundtable.

International Standard Book Number-13: 978-0-309-72695-5
International Standard Book Number-10: 0-309-72695-6
Digital Object Identifier: https://doi.org/10.17226/27976

This publication is available from the National Academies Press, 500 Fifth Street, NW, Keck 360, Washington, DC 20001; (800) 624-6242; http://www.nap.edu.

Copyright 2025 by the National Academy of Sciences. National Academies of Sciences, Engineering, and Medicine and National Academies Press and the graphical logos for each are all trademarks of the National Academy of Sciences. All rights reserved.

Printed in the United States of America.

Suggested citation: National Academies of Sciences, Engineering, and Medicine. 2025. *National Science, Technology, and Security Roundtable Capstone: Proceedings of a Workshop*. Washington, DC: National Academies Press. https://doi.org/10.17226/27976.

The **National Academy of Sciences** was established in 1863 by an Act of Congress, signed by President Lincoln, as a private, nongovernmental institution to advise the nation on issues related to science and technology. Members are elected by their peers for outstanding contributions to research. Dr. Marcia McNutt is president.

The **National Academy of Engineering** was established in 1964 under the charter of the National Academy of Sciences to bring the practices of engineering to advising the nation. Members are elected by their peers for extraordinary contributions to engineering. Dr. John L. Anderson is president.

The **National Academy of Medicine** (formerly the Institute of Medicine) was established in 1970 under the charter of the National Academy of Sciences to advise the nation on medical and health issues. Members are elected by their peers for distinguished contributions to medicine and health. Dr. Victor J. Dzau is president.

The three Academies work together as the **National Academies of Sciences, Engineering, and Medicine** to provide independent, objective analysis and advice to the nation and conduct other activities to solve complex problems and inform public policy decisions. The National Academies also encourage education and research, recognize outstanding contributions to knowledge, and increase public understanding in matters of science, engineering, and medicine.

Learn more about the National Academies of Sciences, Engineering, and Medicine at **www.nationalacademies.org**.

Consensus Study Reports published by the National Academies of Sciences, Engineering, and Medicine document the evidence-based consensus on the study's statement of task by an authoring committee of experts. Reports typically include findings, conclusions, and recommendations based on information gathered by the committee and the committee's deliberations. Each report has been subjected to a rigorous and independent peer-review process and it represents the position of the National Academies on the statement of task.

Proceedings published by the National Academies of Sciences, Engineering, and Medicine chronicle the presentations and discussions at a workshop, symposium, or other event convened by the National Academies. The statements and opinions contained in proceedings are those of the participants and are not endorsed by other participants, the planning committee, or the National Academies.

Rapid Expert Consultations published by the National Academies of Sciences, Engineering, and Medicine are authored by subject-matter experts on narrowly focused topics that can be supported by a body of evidence. The discussions contained in rapid expert consultations are considered those of the authors and do not contain policy recommendations. Rapid expert consultations are reviewed by the institution before release.

For information about other products and activities of the National Academies, please visit www.nationalacademies.org/about/whatwedo.

PLANNING COMMITTEE FOR THE NATIONAL SCIENCE, TECHNOLOGY, AND SECURITY ROUNDTABLE CAPSTONE WORKSHOP

KATHRYN A. MOLER (*Chair*), Marvin Chodorow Professor, and Professor of Applied Physics, of Physics, and of Energy Science and Engineering, Stanford University
THOMAS E. MASON, Director, Los Alamos National Laboratory
J. MICHAEL McQUADE, Special Advisor to the President, Carnegie Mellon University (*until June 30, 2024*)
ANNA PUGLISI, Visiting Fellow, Hoover Institution (*as of September 1, 2024*)

Staff

KARLA HAGAN, Staff Director
STEVEN KENDALL, Senior Program Officer
ZARIYA BUTLER, Senior Program Assistant

NATIONAL SCIENCE, TECHNOLOGY, AND SECURITY ROUNDTABLE

JOHN C. GANNON (*Co-Chair*), Former Chairman, National Intelligence Council (retired)
RICHARD A. MESERVE (*Co-Chair*), President Emeritus, Carnegie Institution
MARIA T. ZUBER (*Co-Chair*), E. A. Griswold Professor of Geophysics, Massachusetts Institute of Technology
CHAOUKI T. ABDALLAH, Executive Vice President for Research and Professor of Electrical and Computer Engineering, Georgia Institute of Technology (*until September 10, 2024*)
CHRISTOPHER AUSTIN, CEO-Partner, Flagship Pioneering (*until March 31, 2024*)
THOMAS FINGAR, Shorenstein APARC Fellow, Freeman Spogli Institute for International Studies, Stanford University
J. MICHAEL McQUADE, Special Advisor to the President, Carnegie Mellon University (*until June 30, 2024*)
KATHRYN A. MOLER, Marvin Chodorow Professor and Professor of Applied Physics, of Physics, and of Energy Science and Engineering, Stanford University
ANNA PUGLISI, Visiting Fellow, Hoover Institution (*as of September 1, 2024*)
JASON DONOVAN (Ex Officio Member), Director of the Office of Science and Technology Cooperation, U.S. Department of State
LYRIC A. JORGENSON (Ex Officio Member), Associate Director for Science Policy, U.S. National Institutes of Health
REBECCA KEISER (Ex Officio Member), Chief of Research Security Strategy and Policy, U.S. National Science Foundation
HARRIET KUNG (Ex Officio Member), Acting Director of the Office of Science, U.S. Department of Energy
MICHAEL S. LAUER (Ex Officio Member), Deputy Director for Extramural Research, U.S. National Institutes of Health
THOMAS E. MASON (Ex Officio Member), Director, Los Alamos National Laboratory
BINDU NAIR (Ex Officio Member), Director for Basic Research, U.S. Department of Defense (*until October 18, 2024*)
JEFFREY J. WELSER (Consultant), Chief Operating Officer, IBM Research

Staff

KARLA HAGAN, Staff Director
STEVEN KENDALL, Senior Program Officer
ZARIYA BUTLER, Senior Program Assistant

Reviewers

This Proceedings of a Workshop was reviewed in draft form by individuals chosen for their diverse perspectives and technical expertise. The purpose of this independent review is to provide candid and critical comments that will assist the National Academies of Sciences, Engineering, and Medicine in making each published proceedings as sound as possible and to ensure that it meets the institutional standards for quality, objectivity, evidence, and responsiveness to the charge. The review comments and draft manuscript remain confidential to protect the integrity of the process.

We thank the following individuals for their review of this proceedings:

THOMAS FINGAR, Stanford University
GIGI KWIK GRONVALL, Johns Hopkins University
KATHRYN A. MOLER, Stanford University
CAROLINE S. WAGNER, The Ohio State University
KATHERINE A. YELICK, University of California, Berkeley

Although the reviewers listed above provided many constructive comments and suggestions, they were not asked to endorse the content of the proceedings nor did they see the final draft before its release. The review of this proceedings was overseen by **E. WILLIAM COLGLAZIER**, American Association for the Advancement of Science (retired). He was responsible for making certain that an independent examination of this proceedings was carried out in accordance with standards of the National Academies and that all review comments were carefully considered. Responsibility for the final content rests entirely with the rapporteur and the National Academies.

Contents

Acronyms and Abbreviations		xiii
Preface		xv
Summary		1
1	Introduction	9
2	The Work of the National Science, Technology, and Security Roundtable	13
3	The U.S. Research System's Role in National and Economic Security	19
4	The Nature of the Geopolitical Challenge	25
5	University and National Lab Responses on Research Security	29
6	Funding Agency Responses	35
7	Law Enforcement Agency Responses	45
8	Legislative, Regulatory, and Other Types of Responses	51
9	Potential Near- and Long-Term Responses on Research Security	57
10	Possible Future Directions for Securing Scientific Research While Preserving Openness in the U.S. Research System	65

11 Concluding Session: A Brief Summary and Synthesis of the
    Capstone Workshop   71

APPENDIXES

A   Abbreviated Agendas for NSTSR Regional Meetings   73
B   Workshop Agenda   85
C   Workshop Advance Reading Materials   91
D   Workshop Slide Presentations   93
E   Biographical Sketches of Workshop Participants   95
F   The National Science, Technology, and Security Roundtable
    Co-Chairs' Paper   113

Acronyms and Abbreviations

AI	artificial intelligence
CIA	U.S. Central Intelligence Agency
CUI	Controlled Unclassified Information
DARPA	Defense Advanced Research Projects Agency
DNI	Director of National Intelligence
DOD	U.S. Department of Defense
DOE	U.S. Department of Energy
DOJ	U.S. Department of Justice
FBI	U.S. Federal Bureau of Investigation
FFRDC	federally funded research and development center
IP	Intellectual Property
IT	Information Technology
NDEA	National Defense Education Act of 1958
NIH	U.S. National Institutes of Health
NSBAC	National Security Business Alliance Council
NSDD-189	National Security Decision Directive 189
NSF	U.S. National Science Foundation
NSHEAB	National Security Higher Education Advisory Board

NSPM-33	National Security Presidential Memorandum – 33
NSTC	National Science and Technology Council
NSTSR	National Science, Technology, and Security Roundtable
OSTP	White House Office of Science and Technology Policy
PI	principal investigator
R&D	research and development
RTES	Research, Technology, and Economic Security
S&T	science and technology
SECURE	Safeguarding the Entire Community in the U.S. Research Ecosystem
STEM	science, technology, engineering, and mathematics
TRUST	Trusted Research Using Safeguards and Transparency

Preface

Since 2020, the National Science, Technology, and Security Roundtable, or NSTSR, has explored the risks and benefits of open research in the context of national and economic security. This capstone workshop brought together experts and stakeholders to reflect on the Roundtable's work and possible paths forward.

An experimental physicist, I began to grapple with research security policy in 2018 when I accepted a role as Stanford University's senior research officer. I joined the national discourse on security and foreign interference just as federal agencies were publicizing research integrity issues, strengthening disclosure requirements, and tightening enforcement. I was sobered by the strong polarization of opinions. Some advocated for the value of the free exchange of ideas but downplayed the costs of unfair practices and resisted increased oversight. Others sounded alarms about threats posed by foreign adversaries but seemed to minimize the disadvantages of restricting research collaboration.

The roundtable gave many stakeholders an opportunity to learn, teach, and promote best practices. We need a common understanding of costs, benefits, and risks: if we ignore the risks, others may unfairly exploit our open system; if we compromise our core strengths, we may sacrifice our inherent advantages.

The roundtable's co-chairs, John Gannon, Dick Meserve, and Maria Zuber, memorialized insights from our conversations and regional visits in a paper shared at the beginning of the capstone workshop and published herein as Appendix F. In the context of the threat from China, they recommended that we weigh the risks of both threats and constraints, welcome and value foreign-born researchers who are eager to join and strengthen our institutions, invest strongly in science and technology, and maintain close contacts between the research community, the funding agencies, and the Intelligence Community.

The planning committee designed this capstone workshop to disseminate and build upon the co-chairs' paper, share the roundtable's work, and discuss ways to address foreign threats and ensure our nation's continued leadership in science and technology. The assembled experts offered valuable perspectives and insights on simultaneously cultivating a thriving research system and safeguarding it through carefully considered security measures.

As I reflect on everything I have learned, four principles emerge:

Differentiate research topics and apply appropriate controls. Agency staff who understand both the science and the tradeoffs should be empowered to make these determinations. Our open research environment accelerates innovation, promotes education, creates opportunities for diplomacy, and broadens our knowledge. We must preserve these benefits while ensuring that open research is conducted with integrity, reciprocity, and transparency. We also must identify research that poses a specific benefit or threat to national security and conduct it in secure environments.

Invest in research. We need to invest sufficiently to remain at the forefront of discovery. Federal funding has declined as a percentage of gross domestic product. The United States still invests substantially in research and development, but our relative global position has slipped as other countries, particularly in Asia, have increased their investments.

Foster talent. As Susan Gordon[1] said during the capstone workshop, the great supply chain issue of our time is not microchips, but talent. The best way we can tackle momentous challenges is to cultivate a smart, creative, and capable new generation, drawing both from domestic and immigrant sources.

Continue sharing expertise and knowledge. The roundtable convened researchers, policymakers, diplomats, faculty members, congressional staffers, national security experts, leaders of technology companies, representatives of professional societies, officials of federal funding agencies,

---

[1] Co-chair of the National Academies of Sciences, Engineering, and Medicine's Committee on Protecting Critical Technologies for National Security in an Era of Openness and Competition and the consensus study report Protecting U.S. Technological Advantage, and former principal deputy director of national intelligence.

scholars in science policy and international relations, experts on intellectual property and export controls, members of the national intelligence and law enforcement communities, administrators and research officers from universities and national labs, individuals affected by government actions both in China and in the United States, and members of the public. When we value and respect each other's expertise, we can develop effective and balanced solutions to the complex challenges that arise wherever science, technology, and national security intersect.

On behalf of the panelists and participants of the capstone workshop, and on behalf of the Workshop Planning Committee consisting of Thom Mason, Michael McQuade, Anna Puglisi, and myself, staffed by Karla Hagan, I hope these proceedings introduce you to issues before us and suggest paths to a secure, strong, and innovative research environment.

> Kathryn A. Moler, *Chair*
> Planning Committee for the National Science, Technology, and Security Roundtable Capstone Workshop

Summary

The National Academies of Sciences, Engineering, and Medicine's National Science, Technology, and Security Roundtable (NSTSR) was called for in the Fiscal Year 2020 National Defense Authorization Act[1] to bring together individuals from federal research agencies, intelligence, law enforcement, academic research, and business communities to explore critical issues related to protecting U.S. national and economic security while ensuring the open exchange of ideas and the international talent required for American leadership in science and technology (S&T).

Between November 2020 and May 2024, the NSTSR held a total of 14 meetings.[2] These included regional meetings around the United States where the NSTSR engaged with researchers, institutions, national laboratories, and industry representatives to gather information and perspectives on a range of issues pertaining to research security.[3] Regional meetings were

---

[1] National Defense Authorization Act for Fiscal Year 2020, P.L. 116-92, Section 1746(b).

[2] For NSTSR and regional meeting agendas from 2020 to 2024, see https://www.dropbox.com/home/NSTSR%20Capstone%20Workshop%20July%2016-17%2C%202024/NSTSR%20Meeting%20Agendas%202020-2024.

[3] The U.S. government defines research security as "safeguarding the research enterprise against the misappropriation of research and development to the detriment of national or economic security, related violations of research integrity, and foreign government interference." See Joint Committee on the Research Environment Subcommittee on Research Security, *Guidance for Implementing National Security Presidential Memorandum 33 (NSPM-33) on National Security Strategy for United States Government-Supported Research and Development*, January 2022, p. 24.

held at the University of Maryland, Massachusetts Institute of Technology, Northwestern University, Hoover Institution at Stanford University, and Texas A&M University (see Appendix A for abbreviated agendas of NSTSR regional meetings). The NSTSR also convened a workshop on November 14 and 15, 2022, entitled *Openness, International Engagement, and the Federally Funded Science and Technology Research Enterprise*.[4]

Since the first meeting of the NSTSR in 2020, there have been numerous discussions around the topic of research security among policymakers and affected communities, and the policy landscape has continued to evolve. The NSTSR played a role in these discussions, and to capture what was learned and explore potential future directions before the NSTSR sunsets in late 2024, a Capstone Workshop was held on July 16 and 17, 2024. Discussions over the 2 days of the workshop included observations by participants about the nature of the challenge of research security in the United States, reflections on actions that the United States has taken on research security to date, and possible future directions.

Because it was a roundtable and not a consensus study committee, the NSTSR's mandate did not include making consensus recommendations. The three co-chairs authored a paper with their personal conclusions and recommendations, which was provided to attendees in advance of the workshop and is included in Appendix F. In addition to the co-chairs' paper, this volume provides a summary of the many viewpoints expressed by members of the NSTSR and other workshop participants. More detail on presenters' views can be found in the slides from the workshop in Appendix D.

This proceedings was prepared by a rapporteur as a factual summary of the presentations and discussions that took place at the workshop. It does not necessarily represent the positions of the workshop participants as a whole, the planning committee, the NSTSR, or the National Academies of Sciences, Engineering, and Medicine, and should not be construed as reflecting any group consensus.

THE NATURE OF THE CHALLENGE

Research plays a critical role in U.S. national and economic security. As was noted repeatedly by participants during the workshop, the challenge

---

[4] For Proceedings in Brief from the NSTSR workshop *Openness, International Engagement, and the Federally Funded Science and Technology Research Enterprise*, see https://nap.nationalacademies.org/catalog/27091/openness-international-engagement-and-the-federally-funded-science-and-technology-research-enterprise.

facing the nation is how to implement policies and procedures ensuring that the national and economic security of the United States is adequately protected and enhanced by the right balance of research openness and research security. Maintaining the preeminence of the U.S. research system in an era where some countries engage in practices that take unfair advantage of open aspects of our research system in a non-reciprocal, non-transparent way has become a significant issue for the United States.

The People's Republic of China raises the most significant challenge, according to many participants, because it has become a near-peer competitor in science, technology, and innovation, many of its scientists engage with American scientists, and its government has employed practices, including stealing intellectual property and espionage, that are not compatible with the values and practices that underpin the open aspects of the U.S. research ecosystem. Relations between the United States and Chinese governments have become highly adversarial across a range of issues, many noted. China has stated S&T ambitions to outcompete the United States and has developed a whole-of-system approach, devoting considerable resources to building a robust and high performing research ecosystem for advancing its national interests.

An important element of the challenge, according to many workshop participants, is that the United States no longer enjoys preeminence in either investments or in achievements in many important and strategic areas of research—a sentiment echoed by subject matter experts reflecting on their own fields of research during NSTSR's regional meetings around the United States. A number of participants in the regional meetings suggested that with a thoughtful approach, the United States can preserve important aspects of its open research system that benefit the country while also ensuring that the system protects and enhances U.S. national and economic security.

COLLABORATING INTERNATIONALLY

U.S. values such as openness and scientific rigor are a strength, most participants observed, adding that it is important to fortify and uphold those values when conducting research, including international scientific collaboration. Collaborating internationally in research is crucial to advancing research, many participants said, but it is also necessary to be cognizant of others' values when doing so, and caution should be applied when values relating to transparency, reciprocity, and accountability are not shared. Some workshop participants pointed out that even our well-aligned allies have different policies than the United States regarding security and openness. One participant questioned assumptions about trust in scientific research activities, suggesting that not all collaborations can be built around an assumption of mutual trust.

APPROACHES TO RESEARCH SECURITY

An all-of-system approach is the best way to maintain both U.S. national security and preeminence in science and technology, many participants said, with some saying that the U.S. approach up to now has been tactical and has not appropriately considered the entire S&T system. Many noted that National Security Presidential Memorandum – 33[5] provided an important platform from which to launch research security efforts in the United States, but that it is just a start.

Most participants called for a flexible, risk-based approach to allow the United States to leverage the gains in scientific research that arise from an open research environment with robust international collaboration, while at the same time protecting the most sensitive work. Many advocated for a risk management approach where both risks and benefits are evaluated and prioritized, considering not only the personnel involved in a particular proposed research project but also the specific topic of the research. Institutions will not all implement the same risk management approach, some participants noted, because different institutions have different risk profiles. For example, some universities perform classified work on their campuses, while other universities do not.

For analyzing a proposed federally funded research project, the balance between preserving openness and protecting sensitive work can be achieved through a process of carefully identifying and categorizing sensitive information. Federal funding agencies shared their different approaches to categorizing and making decisions regarding sensitive projects during the workshop. These approaches vary according to varying federal agency missions, and the workshop included detailed presentations of the methodologies that are being applied by the U.S. Department of Defense, Department of Energy, National Institutes of Health, and

---

[5] The White House. 2021. "Presidential Memorandum on United States Government-Supported Research and Development National Security Policy." National Security Presidential Memorandum – 33 (NSPM-33), January 14, 2021.

National Science Foundation. However, though these approaches vary, many workshop participants cautioned that the U.S. government should nonetheless seek harmonization of federal science-funding agencies' policies on research security to the maximum extent possible—a sentiment echoed by the academic community during NSTSR regional meetings around the country.

Some participants pointed out concerns from researchers about lack of clarity on what type of international collaboration is acceptable by federal agencies and what type is prohibited, a concern that the NSTSR heard from researchers and university research security leads at its regional meetings.

To aid with the exchange of information, productive relationships between the research community and the law enforcement and intelligence communities are key. Many have worked to develop such relationships, and the result has been increased understanding and trust between these communities, which can, in turn, foster the development of a mutually reinforcing system for achieving research security. Several participants emphasized that having individuals with technical and security expertise as a trusted part of the research system is key to being able to make security decisions on potential collaborative work on a case-by-case basis.

INVESTMENTS IN SCIENTIFIC RESEARCH AND TALENT

A key theme highlighted by many participants is that achieving U.S. national security requires not only protective measures but also investment to boost open, fundamental scientific research. They felt that the United States can win the current nation-state competition by "running faster" in S&T, but only if it makes the needed investments. This includes investments in talent and developing a workforce sufficient to meet the needs of the U.S. S&T enterprise.

DISCUSSION OF NEXT STEPS FOR ACHIEVING RESEARCH SECURITY WHILE MAINTAINING U.S. PREEMINENCE

Several possible next steps in achieving research security while maintaining U.S. S&T preeminence were proposed, including the development of a comprehensive U.S. science, technology, and security strategy, and a strategy for the recruitment, retention, and development of talent. Some participants suggested that new legislation is needed to boost education in

STEM (science, technology, engineering, and mathematics), for example an updated National Defense Education Act.[6]

One participant expressed concern about a lack of societal understanding of the value S&T provides to the U.S. economy and national security and for why we have our S&T system in the first place, suggesting that there should be more efforts to educate the public about the importance of the U.S. S&T system to our prosperity and security and the critical roles that open scientific research, international collaboration, and talent recruitment play in U.S. success.

Some participants felt that U.S. global preeminence and leadership in S&T is diminishing and challenged by factors that are more important to address than countering malign actions by certain foreign actors. From this point of view, it would be a mistake to think that stopping bad actors is sufficient for restoring and maintaining U.S. preeminence. Many noted that increasing investments in S&T is crucial to ensure U.S. technological preeminence and outcompete foreign adversaries.

Many participants argued that investment in U.S. talent and research capabilities is necessary but not sufficient, and that to maintain preeminence, the United States must also avoid counterproductive measures that might stifle research and preclude participation in the S&T enterprise by smaller research institutions.

Several participants noted that working with international governments and institutions of partners, allies, and like-minded countries to address research security concerns will make the U.S. and global response to threats from foreign interference more effective. Vetting foreign individuals seeking to work or study in the United States was also discussed, with participants expressing different views on whether such vetting should be undertaken in the government or at research institutions.

Even without the People's Republic of China, there would still be challenges to achieving research security, and many participants suggested that policies should not be adopted exclusively to counter China. The U.S. government recognizes threats to research security coming from other countries, identified in some government policies as "countries of concern," including Russia, North Korea, and Iran.[7] Several workshop participants

---

[6] See Chapter 9 for discussion of the National Defense Education Act at the Capstone Workshop.

[7] For example, the CHIPS and Science Act indicates that "foreign countries of concern" related to malign foreign talent recruitment programs include the People's Republic of China, the Democratic People's Republic of Korea, the Russian Federation, and the Islamic Republic of Iran. See P.L. 117-167, Section 10612(a)(1).

also cautioned to avoid overly focusing on any one particular country in efforts to achieve research security, citing that countries of concern in the future may include countries not currently on this list.

During the course of the NSTSR's convenings, concerns were expressed by Chinese and Chinese American scholars about what seemed to be ethnic targeting by the U.S. government of Chinese and Chinese American researchers working in the United States. Many workshop participants cautioned against reinstating the Department of Justice's China Initiative,[8] as it was a policy that was not effective at addressing the problem of research security, was overly focused on China when threats now and in the future will also come from elsewhere, and unnecessarily stoked ethnic divisions in the United States.

Controlled Unclassified Information (CUI) was a topic of particular concern during the workshop and throughout the NSTSR's convenings, with participants urging that CUI restrictions not be applied excessively, that the application of CUI be consistent across federal agencies, and that the creation of new categories of CUI be avoided.

Improved understanding of foreign threats to the U.S. research system would provide needed analysis and quantification of the problem, according to many participants. Issues identified as requiring a deeper understanding were: how often ethical violations due to foreign interference occur in open research, what the impacts of those ethical violations are, and the scale and impact of foreign interference in federally funded versus private-sector funded research and development (R&D). It was also seen as important to assess the costs and benefits of performing R&D in a restricted versus an open setting.

Many participants observed that it will be important to have a forum where academia, the private sector, federal research funding agencies, intelligence agencies, and law enforcement would be able to continue to come together for ongoing discussions to share information on research security threats and risks.

---

[8] See Chapters 7, 8, and 10 and the NSTSR co-chairs' paper in Appendix F for more discussion of the Department of Justice's China Initiative.

1

Introduction

The National Academies of Sciences, Engineering, and Medicine's National Science, Technology, and Security Roundtable (NSTSR) was called for in the Fiscal Year 2020 National Defense Authorization Act[1] to bring together individuals from federal research agencies, intelligence, law enforcement, academic research, and business communities to explore critical issues related to protecting U.S. national and economic security while ensuring the open exchange of ideas and the international talent required for American leadership in science and technology (S&T). The NSTSR's original charge can be found in its Statement of Task in Box 1-1. The NSTSR's discussions evolved to focus on security threats resulting from the open and collaborative nature of research and efforts by foreign actors to exploit federally funded research using illicit methods. The NSTSR also broadened the scope of its work beyond the focus on research security in the Statement of Task to include challenges facing U.S. global preeminence in S&T and ways to enhance U.S. S&T capabilities and competitiveness.

Between November 2020 and May 2024, the NSTSR held a total of 14 meetings. These included regional meetings around the United States where the NSTSR engaged with researchers, institutions, national laboratories, and industry representatives in the region to gather information and perspectives on a range of issues pertaining to research security

---

[1] National Defense Authorization Act for Fiscal Year 2020, P.L. 116-92, Section 1746(b).

> **BOX 1-1**
> **National Science, Technology, and Security Roundtable Statement of Task**
>
> The open exchange of scientific and technical information has long been a fundamental tenet of science and an important feature of academic and federally funded research in the United States. Recent reports of foreign governments acquiring information and materials from foreign students and faculty studying and working in U.S. institutions and from U.S. faculty engaged in collaborative research activities abroad are raising concerns that the open exchange of U.S. scientific and technical know-how may be presenting new national and economic security risks in an increasingly global and competitive environment. The National Academies of Sciences, Engineering, and Medicine will establish a National Science, Technology, and Security Roundtable to provide a neutral venue where individuals from the national intelligence and law enforcement communities can meet with representatives from industry and the academic research community to discuss current threats, benefits, and potential risks. The roundtable will (1) explore critical issues related to protecting U.S. national and economic security; (2) identify and consider security threats and risks associated with federally funded research and development; (3) identify effective approaches to communicating threats and risks; (4) share best practices for addressing and mitigating the threats and risks; and (5) examine potential near- and long-term responses by stakeholders in the research enterprise to mitigate and address the risks associated with foreign threats. Proceedings of the roundtable discussions will be produced as will an overarching summary at the end of 4 years.

(see Appendix A for abbreviated agendas of NSTSR regional meetings). Regional meetings were held at the University of Maryland, Massachusetts Institute of Technology, Northwestern University, Hoover Institution at Stanford University, and Texas A&M University.[2] The NSTSR also convened a workshop on November 14 and 15, 2022, entitled *Openness,*

---

[2] For NSTSR and regional meeting agendas from 2020 to 2024, see https://www.dropbox.com/home/NSTSR%20Capstone%20Workshop%20July%2016-17%2C%202024/NSTSR%20Meeting%20Agendas%202020-2024.

INTRODUCTION   11

International Engagement, and the Federally Funded Science and Technology Research Enterprise.[3]

On July 16 and 17, 2024, an ad hoc committee under the auspices of the National Academies convened a Capstone Workshop in Washington, D.C.,[4] which served as the culmination of the NSTSR's 4 years of convenings. The Capstone Workshop focused on national security issues resulting from the way in which federally funded research is conducted in the United States, efforts to exploit the open research ecosystem, and ways to mitigate risks. The workshop was structured to highlight how different stakeholders perceive threats to the U.S. S&T ecosystem, what has been done to address threats, and what should be done. The workshop also focused on things the United States should do to enhance our S&T capabilities and global competitiveness.

The workshop included panels on the work of the NSTSR; the U.S. research system's role in national and economic security; the evolution of university and national lab responses on research security; the evolution of funding agency responses on research security; the evolution of law enforcement agency responses on research security; the nature of the geopolitical challenge; legislative, regulatory, and other types of responses on research security; and potential near- and long-term responses on research security.

Members of the NSTSR served as moderators for panel sessions, with each having the option to provide their perspectives from their 4 years of work with the roundtable during the session. Panel presentations were followed by discussion. At the end of the workshop, members of the NSTSR offered concluding reflections on issues of U.S. national security and the U.S. S&T ecosystem.

The NSTSR Capstone Workshop was organized by a planning committee whose role was limited to identification of topics and speakers. This *Proceedings of the Capstone Workshop* was prepared by a rapporteur as a factual summary of the presentations and discussions that took place at the workshop. Statements, recommendations, and opinions expressed are those of individual presenters and participants and do not necessarily represent

---

[3] For Proceedings in Brief from the NSTSR workshop Openness, International Engagement, and the Federally Funded Science and Technology Research Enterprise, see https://nap.nationalacademies.org/catalog/27091/openness-international-engagement-and-the-federally-funded-science-and-technology-research-enterprise.

[4] See Appendixes B–E for the Capstone Workshop agenda, advance reading materials, slide presentations, and biographies for Capstone Workshop participants.

the positions of the workshop participants as a whole, the planning committee, or the National Academies, and should not be construed as reflecting any group consensus.

2

The Work of the National Science, Technology, and Security Roundtable

Co-chairs Richard Meserve (formerly of the Carnegie Institution), John Gannon (formerly of the National Intelligence Council), and Maria Zuber (Massachusetts Institute of Technology) summarized the 4 years of work of the National Science, Technology, and Security Roundtable (NSTSR), drawing upon a paper that they drafted.[1]

Meserve began by discussing the challenges to open science and fundamental research, highlighting that the encouragement of open, international involvement in basic science is important and powerful. Foreign-born workers are an essential ingredient to the U.S. research enterprise. Nineteen percent of workers in U.S. STEM (science, technology, engineering, and mathematics) fields at the bachelor's degree level are foreign born, and more than half in some critical fields such as computer science and mathematics at the doctorate level are foreign born.[2] Meserve acknowledged concerns that foreign researchers could develop skills that could be used to the detriment of the United States. However, many foreign students who come to the United States for training remain. Stay rates are 88 percent after 5 years and 81 percent after 10 years for science and engineering doctorate recip-

---

[1] See Appendix F for the paper submitted to the Capstone Workshop by NSTSR Co-Chairs John C. Gannon, Richard A. Meserve, and Maria T. Zuber. This paper was circulated to workshop participants prior to the workshop.

[2] NSB, NSF (National Science Board, National Science Foundation). 2024. *Science and Engineering Indicators 2024: The State of U.S. Science and Engineering.* NSB-2024-3. Alexandria, VA. https://ncses.nsf.gov/pubs/nsb20243/talent-u-s-and-global-stem-education-and-labor-force.

13

> "A strengthened process is needed to weigh both the threat to our economic and national security arising from openness and the risk to research competitiveness by constraining openness."
> Richard Meserve
> Carnegie Institution (formerly)

ients with Chinese citizenship at graduation.[3] This "brain drain" to the United States gives us strength, as native U.S.-born talent is not available in sufficient numbers to meet needs. Discouraging foreign involvement in U.S. science is counterproductive, Meserve said.

Meserve added that, over the last 4 years, great progress has been made in meeting the challenge of achieving research security while also preserving openness. He identified additional items for consideration for the future:

1. *A rigorous, risk-informed approach is key.* While Meserve recognized the need for more scrutiny in critical areas, "a strengthened process is needed to weigh both the threat to our economic and national security arising from openness and the risk to research competitiveness by constraining openness."
2. *Restrictions should be imposed on the application of Controlled Unclassified Information (CUI).* There has been a proliferation of restrictions imposed by federal agencies to control the public release of information. CUI designations should be limited to instances where a substantial threat to national and economic security exists and the risks from openness can be convincingly shown to exceed the benefits of collaboration. At the very least, the CUI designation should be revisited by the government with the objective of limiting its scope, achieving consistency in application, and providing clear guidance on how to handle sensitive information. In cases where a restriction is applied, researchers and the federal funding agency should allow open research to proceed if the researcher and the funding agency reach agreement on measures to mitigate risk, such as agreement to restrict dissemination of information relating to limited aspects of the work.
3. *It is important to take special care to reassure foreign-born researchers that they are welcome and valued.* Foreign-born researchers

---

[3] NSB, NSF, *Science and Engineering Indicators 2024.*

are essential contributors to our science and technology (S&T) enterprise. The U.S. government should respond forcefully to continuing cases of discrimination and harassment, including alleged harassment of traveling students and faculty at U.S. borders.
4. *The close working relationship between government and the research community in developing the National Security Presidential Memorandum – 33 (NSPM-33) should serve as a model for future engagement between the communities.*[4]
5. *The success of our S&T system is dependent on providing necessary resources.* We should not feel that we have responded to the international challenge to our system unless we devote the necessary resources to strengthen U.S. capability.

Gannon summarized the evolution of collaboration between academia and law enforcement during the roundtable's tenure, saying that the United States has made progress toward better collaboration between law enforcement and the scientific community on achieving research security. But we continue to need help from the rest of government and, in some cases, the rest of the world. He said that China is a major threat both in counterintelligence and in scientific research, Russia is a formidable (but distant) second, and Iran and North Korea have also worked against us in significant ways. There is a growing awareness of the foreign threat to research security, especially from China. Research agencies have increased their defenses, and universities "on their own or in cooperation with NSPM-33, have developed strong risk management processes" that need to be strengthened and extended across the research enterprise, according to Gannon.

> "Counterintelligence is important, but science is more important with regard to investing in research capabilities to compete with China."
>
> John Gannon
> National Intelligence Council (formerly)

The NSTSR learned how regional collaboration between universities could be achieved to beneficial effect, according to Gannon. The Federal

---

[4] The White House. 2021. "Presidential Memorandum on United States Government-Supported Research and Development National Security Policy." National Security Presidential Memorandum – 33 (NSPM-33), January 14, 2021.

Bureau of Investigation (FBI) is not just putting demands on researchers but are also working with universities to improve delivery of intelligence on threats and to build capabilities to strengthen universities' ability to achieve research security against foreign interference. During the course of its convenings, the NSTSR heard that the research community is willing to accept guidance on research security. However, Gannon said that the research community still wants more explanation on threats and actions required by the federal government, which he asserted was a healthy sign and exhibits the need for continued communication and deeper collaboration.

Gannon advocated for a whole-of-government approach to research security, which he asserted is needed to counter a foreign threat that includes China's immense capacity in cyber operations. We need a national S&T strategy that integrates science and security throughout the policy formulation and implementation process, including at the start. This is doable, but not yet achieved, according to Gannon, who encouraged NSTSR members individually and collectively to engage in the larger debate to influence the outcome for a more forceful defense of open science.

The major challenge from China is in its growing global competitiveness in scientific research, Gannon stated, and not in its illicit and disruptive interference with U.S. research. He added that, independent of the well-documented threats from China, Russia, Iran, and North Korea entirely, broader foreign interference exists and will persist because of the interconnectedness of global research and development today and the erosion of the United States' foreign leadership position that it once held. The United States must work collaboratively with our allies to restore and strengthen the U.S.-inspired rules in a compliance-based open resource system.

The NSTSR noted continuing concern about reports of security breaches in academia involving international collaboration, mostly related to disclosure failures, but Gannon contended that there were few reported cases of actual espionage involving U.S. universities. According to the Center for Strategic and International Studies,[5] incidents of insider espionage collaboration with China have been few—never more than 10 over a period of 20 years. He added that a large majority of foreign students in our universities are there for educational purposes and not for illicit activities or

---

[5] Center for Strategic and International Studies. 2023. *Survey of Chinese Espionage in the United States Since 2000*. https://www.csis.org/programs/strategic-technologies-program/survey-chinese-espionage-united-states-2000.

espionage, and that the FBI supports this judgement.[6] The NSTSR heard from universities that universities must do more to reassure foreign students that their value is appreciated and their contributions are recognized.

Zuber provided an overview of the evolving response of research universities on research security issues. The NSTSR decided to focus on universities early in its work, because of the open nature of research in universities and because the U.S. government is a major funder of academic research and therefore has a measure of oversight over institutions. The NSTSR heard that significant progress has been made in containing the threat of foreign interference, protecting open science, defending international engagement, and embracing foreign talent. There has been an increase in awareness of the serious and growing threat, and there is little doubt in academia that some foreign countries have nefarious intentions, Zuber said. Research agencies have stepped up and sharpened their defenses, including by developing strong risk management processes and structured research security programs. She noted that it has been helpful for academia to learn from agencies about hundreds of examples of adjudicated cases of violations of research security, because these cases make it clear there is a problem. Among these cases, a small number have been espionage. "The challenge is to take action on the problem while not giving up the benefits of an open research system."

> "If we lock all the doors in our house but don't invest in our research enterprise at the level that maintains our preeminence, then it's hard to see America winning."
> Maria Zuber
> Massachusetts Institute of Technology

Universities are subject to the theft of intellectual property and such theft can result in loss of patent revenue. Zuber emphasized that the "know-how" is very important: details about how to use a certain machine or how to conduct a lab experiment, can take months or even years to develop. The very real possibility of inadvertently welcoming nefarious actors into a lab where they can absorb that know-how is a challenge to our research model. Universities do not want bad actors on their campuses, and Zuber said universities should be able to count on the federal government to flag risks posed by individuals and not issue visas to those individuals. Vetting is

---

[6] Federal Bureau of Investigation. 2019. *China: The Risk to Academia.* https://www.fbi.gov/file-repository/china-risk-to-academia-2019.pdf/view.

a challenge for universities because they are not investigative organizations. Smaller universities do not all have the resources and infrastructure necessary to comply with research security policies, which could present a barrier to participation in the research enterprise and works against broadening the S&T talent pool.

Universities are acting to comply with government regulations, the NSPM-33 guidance, and National Institutes of Health mandates to review lab notebooks,[7] among other efforts. Efforts like digital curriculum vitae and increased diligence at universities and agencies are driving down noncompliance, both inadvertent and purposeful, Zuber said. But there has been a chilling effect for international students, and she has seen hesitance to apply for federal funding by some researchers over concerns about facing arrest if a form is incorrectly filled out inadvertently.

Zuber said that, even if we drive down noncompliance to research security mandates to zero, we will still have a "China problem." If U.S. research security efforts thwart a small number of espionage cases, but in the process further increase the administrative burden for all researchers, this will make U.S. research less competitive. She said that "if we lock all the doors in our house but don't invest in our research enterprise at the level that maintains our preeminence, then it's hard to see America winning."

---

[7] On January 1, 2024, NIH issued policy guidance requiring foreign subaward recipients to provide copies of all lab notebooks, data, and documentation to the U.S.-based grant awardee. For NIH's Policy Guidance for Subaward/Consortium Written Agreements, see https://grants.nih.gov/grants/guide/notice-files/NOT-OD-23-182.html.

3

The U.S. Research System's Role in National and Economic Security

J. Michael McQuade (Carnegie Mellon University), moderator of the workshop's second panel, opened the session by observing that it is important to stop to think about why we are taking action on research security: why science and technology (S&T) matters; what the research ecosystem has done for our country; and the role science and technology plays in bringing about a society that is secure and creates economic growth. McQuade expressed concern that the broader U.S. society does not understand the value of S&T, why expertise and investment in the creation of the future matters, and why we have our S&T system in the first place.

McQuade introduced Susan Gordon (former Principal Deputy Director of National Intelligence) and Patrick Gallagher (University of Pittsburgh), co-chairs of the National Academies of Sciences, Engineering, and Medicine study *Protecting U.S. Technological Advantage*.[1]

Gordon said that the study was originally titled "Protecting U.S. Technology in a Time of Openness," but this was changed because the United States is no longer a leader in every technology. We must protect technology as well as advantage: first, it is important to have something worthy of protecting, and second, you must protect that advantage. Gordon observed that "we've come to a place where every technology is available to everyone, and the advantage will go to the person who puts it to clever use fastest."

---

[1] National Academies of Sciences, Engineering, and Medicine. 2022. *Protecting U.S. Technological Advantage*. Washington, DC: The National Academies Press. https://doi.org/10.17226/26647.

Protecting advantage with a platform like cloud computing or artificial intelligence is different than in other fields.

Gordon noted that much fundamental research is funded by the private sector, over which the federal government has almost no control until a technology is created and utilized, and then it is like "putting genies back in the bottle." Government research funding has decreased as private-sector research funding has increased. However, research in the two sectors is very different. Government has big problems to solve, long-term horizons, and "deep pockets." On the other hand, the private sector operates in commercially expedient ways. Even if the focus of research security actions is universities, it is important to see the whole ecosystem.

> "We've come to a place where every technology is available to everyone, and the advantage will go to the person who puts it to clever use fastest."
> Susan Gordon
> Principal Deputy Director of National Intelligence (formerly)

Gordon said that the great supply chain issue of our time is not microchips, but talent. The United States could harm its advantage if it decouples too much from China. We have an industrial base that is starved for talent, and foreign-born researchers could fill this void. If the United States adopts a strategy of coupling educational opportunities with an opportunity to work in industry, this would provide an advantage that some of our allies and partners do not have because of the size of their talent base.

Gallagher noted significant overlap between the National Science, Technology, and Security Roundtable (NSTSR) co-chairs' paper[2] and the *Protecting U.S. Technological Advantage* study.

For the study, the original charge for the committee was to look at research security with a list of specific technologies to consider. However, the committee broadened the focus by using specific technologies as case studies and including a focus on platform technologies, which are broadly shared and enabling. These platform technologies, for example, artificial intelligence, cloud computation, 5G telecommunications, and synthetic biology, can be adapted for varied uses and are exceedingly difficult to control effectively and appropriately. Gallagher said that in the past, tech-

---

[2] See Chapter 2 for the NSTSR co-chairs' presentation of their paper at the Capstone Workshop. The paper may be found in Appendix F.

nologies tended to be discrete and single-purpose and could be controlled based on that. However, security strategies the United States will need for the technological landscape today, where newer technologies have multiple uses, are "going to look very different than the entire control regime [for discrete technologies] that we've built."

Gallagher said that the United States no longer enjoys sole supremacy in S&T. Many competitors that have "run the American play," reverse-engineered our approach, and are seeing the fruits of their efforts. The U.S. approach is a product of the Cold War, but it is a mistake to see China as equivalent to Cold War Russia. There is a "frenemies" aspect of our engagement with China, and our codependency raises issues not present in the relationships with the Soviet Union and its allies. China is an economically integrated geopolitical adversary, and it does not adhere to what we consider proper international behavior. The National Security Decision Directive 189 (NSDD-189)[3] discusses the advantages of open research, as does the *Protecting U.S. Technological Advantage* study, but this openness also implies an acceptance of a certain amount of risk. However, if the United States has less of an overwhelming advantage than we did when NSDD-189 was issued in the 1980s, how does that change the risk calculus? Gallagher suggested that we have not yet answered that, and that this fact is probably behind the increasing controls on research that we see coming from the U.S. government.

Protecting U.S. Technological Advantage calls for an exercise that will explicitly define the benefits of open science. Gallagher raised a series of questions related to this: What is an "open system"? What does it need to be open to? Who is allowed to be involved? At what point do restrictions have an impact on the open environment?

The report also calls for an all-of-government approach to solve the challenge of protecting our technological advantage. The study committee struggled with who would be responsible for coordinating a U.S. response across the science, research, development, intelligence, and law enforcement communities. Gallagher suggested that some of the actions on protecting U.S. technological advantage belong in Congress, such as immigration and talent, but that many are executive branch responsibilities that cut across multiple agencies.

---

[3] The White House. 1985. "National Policy on the Transfer of Scientific, Technical and Engineering Information." National Security Decision Directive 189 (NSDD-189), September 21, 1985.

Gallagher suggested that the United States is playing all defense and no offense. Risk management has become a discussion only about controls on research. For example, in many cases increasing the support for research might be an effective strategy to address loss of U.S. technological advantage. The intelligence community has an important role to play in the U.S. approach and starts the discussion based on their perspective and concerns. However, the scientific community should also be brought into the discussion.

Gallagher said that talent is the most critical supply chain issue. While the United States has the world's best training environment, particularly for Ph.D.'s, U.S. universities admit many more Ph.D. students than can find employment after graduation, and that foreign students in the United States should not simply be seen as a resource for increasing university productivity. We must adopt a strategy that integrates S&T training, mission, and talent. There are legitimate questions about the practice of training international talent in the United States, then exporting that talent back to its home country where the knowledge gained has the potential to be used against our interests.

DISCUSSION

McQuade opened the discussion by asking how we should engage with the private sector. Gordon said that a "fraught" political environment means that companies are backing off from engaging in discussions on security and S&T. She said there is a large amount of private investment in addressing issues related to U.S. national security disadvantages; however, the focus of this investment is on narrow problems. Further discussion centered on the possibility of increasing U.S. engagement in international standards-setting. Without this, the United States risks being less relevant on the world stage than other players, for example, the European Union.

There was discussion around the supply chain of talent, with Gallagher suggesting that talent is where advantage comes from. Gordon said that "it's a big, scary world out there, but it is also an incredibly opportunistic world" and that what the United States would like to do is be able to operate everywhere securely. She suggested that this means getting government to say what actions it needs, along with industrial partners saying what factors should also be taken into consideration.

Gordon said that those concerned about issues of science and security should engage with incoming U.S. administrations to discuss these issues and work toward more effective, whole-of-government action. She suggested a focus of such engagement should be the "triumvirate" of the Department of Commerce, Department of Defense, and the Intelligence Community. McQuade suggested that both the NSTSR and the *Protecting U.S. Technological Advantage* study argue for a risk-based strategy, adding that risk is not just about what leaks could occur but also includes lack of performance, lack of innovation, and lack of progress.

4

The Nature of the Geopolitical Challenge

Anna Puglisi (Hoover Institution) spoke about the geopolitical challenge from the People's Republic of China, noting that her research led to the creation of the term "nontraditional collector." She said that "there is no room for xenophobia or ethnic profiling in open liberal democracies … it goes against everything we stand for. Precisely because of these values, we must move forward to find principled ways to mitigate the policies of a nation-state that is ever more authoritarian and seeks to undermine the global norms of science and our values." Puglisi added that "extreme policy reactions, such as closing our eyes or closing our doors, only benefit China."

Puglisi discussed how the Chinese research ecosystem works and how it is different from our own. The challenge coming from China is different than what the United States faced during the Cold War. While many assumed that China would become more like the United States as it became richer, this has not been the case. In China, there is a blurring between public and private entities and between civilian and military activities. The Chinese government treats technology and the robust science and technology (S&T) infrastructure needed to develop it as a national asset, however China operates under a different set of ethics than the United States in science and research. China has structured its S&T system in a way that is inherently at odds with global norms of science, which are built on transparency, reciprocity, and sharing.

China's legal system adds complexity to international research collaborations, according to Puglisi, because Chinese laws require citizens to share information and data with the government if asked. This is a requirement regardless of restrictions that others may place on that information and data and, more importantly, who owns it. The Chinese government increasingly intimidates and harshly silences its critics, including its citizens abroad and U.S. citizens who speak out against its policies and systems. Puglisi said that U.S. institutions "were not designed to counter the threat to academic freedom and manipulation of public opinion" posed by China's policies. She added that there is a well-funded propaganda arm in the Chinese government dedicated to the manipulation of public opinion in the United States, which spends hundreds of millions of dollars on these efforts. Some of these propaganda efforts are put toward exacerbating societal tensions in the United States—which the Chinese government understands well—and promoting the idea that any changes in policy are ethnic profiling.

The United States' system is not set up for the current challenge, Puglisi said, because it is focused only on military technologies, the involvement of an intelligence officer, and technology covered under narrow economic espionage statues. Most U.S. policy measures have been tactical and not designed to counter an entire system that is structurally different from our own. Just because something is not prosecutable under laws set up for a different set of challenges, it does not mean that the United States does not have a problem.

> "There is no room for xenophobia or ethnic profiling in open liberal democracies ... it goes against everything we stand for. Precisely because of these values, we must move forward to find principled ways to mitigate the policies of a nation-state that is ever more authoritarian and seeks to undermine the global norms of science and our values."
>
> Anna Puglisi
> Hoover Institution

Puglisi said that the assumption that all international collaboration is good must be questioned. Just as we must find better ways to measure the threat posed by Chinese interference in the United States' S&T ecosystem, we must also find better ways to measure the benefits of international collaboration. More importantly, we need to better understand who benefits. An individual principal investigator can feel like they benefit from a collaboration because they receive funding, students, or postdocs. However, individual benefit does not necessarily translate to institutional or national benefits. Moving forward, the United States needs clear-eyed policies related to China, including ensuring true reciprocity exists in scientific collaborations. There must be repercussions for not complying with S&T agreements, not sharing data, not providing access to foreign facilities, or obfuscating true affiliations of Chinese scientists working in the United States.

The reality facing the United States regarding China is inconvenient to those benefitting in the short term, Puglisi said, including companies looking for short-term profits, academics who personally benefit from funding or cheap labor in their labs, and former government officials who become lobbyists for China's state-owned and state-supported companies. Open democratic societies must have the difficult conversations needed to protect and retain competitiveness and our values. Puglisi added that if we do not "highlight and address policies that violate global norms and our values, we give credence to systems that undermine fairness, openness, and human rights."

DISCUSSION

Jason Donovan (U.S. Department of State) said allies struggle with taking an actor-agnostic approach versus focusing policies on the Chinese Communist Party in particular. Puglisi said that it is essential to work with allies and like-minded countries and that we must acknowledge that China is not a neutral actor. In China, the role of the state is different; Chinese universities, companies, and courts do not act in the same way as they do in the United States.

In response to questions about how science fits into an approach of collaborating when we can, competing when we need to, and being prepared for—but trying to avoid—a conflict, Puglisi said that everything comes down to transparency and reciprocity when engaging in scientific collaborations. She does not agree with others who say that we need China in order to be able to work on global issues of proliferation, climate, and so forth. She recommended that we continue to have dialogues that involve government, civil society, and academia, but that we should be clear-eyed about the fact that China is always working in its own interests.

In response to a question about the feasibility of working only with a closed group of like-minded allies and positioning China on the outside of the scientific community, Puglisi said that she is not advocating that we totally cut off all collaboration with China, underscoring her previous point that extreme policy positions will not help the situation.

5

University and National Lab Responses on Research Security

Chaouki Abdallah (Georgia Institute of Technology) moderated a session that considered the evolution of university and national laboratory responses to research security threats and strategies. The National Science, Technology, and Security Roundtable (NSTSR) sought to understand whether the threat to our research system is qualitatively different from previous threats, or simply larger in size. The conclusion was that the problem is qualitatively different because adversaries have greater resources than in the past. Abdallah called for a "neighborhood watch" approach, where research security is the responsibility of all those working at a university. The security of the United States' science and technology (S&T) system is only as strong as our weakest link; some less-resourced institutions cannot afford to address the challenge of research security, and some international partners and small- and medium-sized companies are not even aware of the issue.

Peter Fisher (Massachusetts Institute of Technology [MIT]) said that he became familiar with research security when the National Science Foundation (NSF) asked JASON, a group of professors that advises the government on matters that are typically classified, to undertake a report on research security in 2019.[1] The report identified research security stakeholders in the research enterprise, which included principal investigators

---

[1] JASON. 2019. *Fundamental Research Security.* https://www.nsf.gov/news/special_reports/jasonsecurity/JSR-19-2IFundamentalResearchSecurity_12062019FINAL.pdf.

(PIs), research leaders, research institutions, professional societies, federal funding agencies, political leadership, and the general public. PIs are key because they set norms for their research groups and how research groups communicate. PIs also recruit, train, and arrange for researcher compensation (including researchers from overseas). Professional societies were also identified as key stakeholders because they provide guidance to PIs based on norms in their particular fields of research.

The authors of the JASON report attempted to create a list of the norms that govern research. However, it was difficult because different S&T fields have different cultures, histories, and perspectives on sharing data and ideas. The report instead identified a set of tools for researchers for assessing engagements in fundamental research. The assessment tools included the questions: Are the terms of the engagement made clear in writing? Have all participants been identified? Are all the participants' conflicts of interest and commitment documented? Is there any aspect of the engagement that seems unusual, unnecessary, or poorly specified?

John Sarrao (SLAC National Accelerator Laboratory), drawing upon his experiences at national laboratories, said that the U.S. research enterprise cannot be effective without international engagement. If we chose not to engage internationally, then we would have nothing worth stealing. However, it is true that real risks exist when others do not share our values. A grand challenge and key priority is to strike an appropriate and dynamic balance between international engagement and research security. Sarrao suggested that we are doing a better job on research security today than we were a couple of years ago and that the NSTSR has played an important role. If we can achieve the right balance, it will do a lot to mitigate the "chill" in international engagements that has been evidenced.

> "We, as a U.S. research enterprise, cannot be successful [without] international engagement. Real risks exist ... when other players in the ecosystem don't share our values. ... The grand challenge is how do we strike that balance appropriately."
>
> John Sarrao
> SLAC National Accelerator Laboratory

In addition to seeking compliance, Sarrao said, the U.S. government must also provide education and awareness regarding research security. Articulating to researchers that the United States' objective is to ensure that researchers' work is protected (and that they get appropriate credit for it) is a powerful lever. We should think about international colleagues as targets of activities carried out by the adversarial governments designed to interfere with the U.S. research system, rather than as threats. Talent is critical to national labs, but the broader research ecosystem is also important because national labs, which are not degree-granting institutions, rely on universities to train talent.

Sarrao said that it is important to focus on protecting the future rather than relitigating the past. Signals about international collaboration from institutional leaders and the government 5 to 10 years ago were very different from today. It is useful to think about research security culture as we think about lab safety culture. Ideally, concerns and issues could be brought forward without fear of reprisal, and there would also be confidence that labs and institutions foster a system of fairness and accountability.

Sarrao said that we must share best practices but recognize that one single approach does not work for all circumstances. Having policies in common across federal agencies for disclosures by those seeking a federal grant are an important starting point. Once commonalities are identified, agencies can tailor disclosure requirements. Every restriction or protection measure comes with an opportunity cost.

It is important to celebrate and communicate the good work we are doing at national labs, Sarrao said, but also to acknowledge that we have much more work to do. He foresees the development of an approach to assess international collaborations in the Department of Energy (DOE) that will bring consistency, transparency, and objectivity by examining the "who," or the affiliation history and role within DOE; the "what," or the scope of the work; and the "where," or acknowledging variability in site access restrictions across laboratories.

Joe Elabd (Texas A&M University System) shared his experiences with research security at the Texas A&M University System. Composed of 11 universities and 8 state agencies, the A&M System is one of the largest in the country, with an enrollment of 157,000 students. It has an annual research portfolio of over $1.5 billion, and it includes a large R1 university, four R2 universities,[2] and a historically Black university.

---

[2] R1 universities are defined as Ph.D.-granting universities with very high research activity, and R2 universities are defined as Ph.D.-granting universities with high research activity, according to the Carnegie Classification of Institutions of Higher Education. See https://carnegieclassifications.acenet.edu/carnegie-classification/classification-methodology/basic-classification/#:~:text=R1%3A%20Doctoral%20Universities%20%E2%80%93%20Very%20high,%2FPU%3A%20Doctoral%2FProfessional%20Universities.

The A&M System has a robust and well-staffed research security program, and smaller universities within the system can make use of systemwide resources. In 2021, A&M performed a systemwide review of international agreements with countries of concern. This review included close to 100 research agreements, academic collaborative agreements, memoranda of understanding, and letters of intent. In-depth risk analyses were performed on each agreement and, as a result, a majority were terminated and the remainder were identified for mitigating measures. A&M found that a significant number of zero-dollar agreements (e.g., foreign exchange programs) were being signed off on by individuals who did not realize that there were risks associated with signing the agreement.

In 2022, A&M instituted a program called High Risk Global Engagements and High Risk International Collaborations, where all foreign engagements are proactively assessed, including travel and co-authorships. Proposed international engagements must be submitted for review to the university's export control officer. Legal, foreign influence, institutional, and reputational risks, among other risks, are evaluated. Reviewers include Elabd as A&M vice chancellor for research and the general counsel. Outcomes of the review include approval, approval with mitigating measures, or denial. About 20 international engagements are reviewed each week. This process has shown the importance of communication and the need for education of faculty researchers, leadership, and the broader community about research security concerns.

DISCUSSION

During discussion, consistency of decision-making across academic institutions on international engagement was raised and panelists expressed the viewpoint that different institutions have different risk profiles. Maria Zuber (MIT) said that risk management policies and procedures should be consistent within an institution, but that safeguards in place for research at universities that perform classified research should be increased compared with those at universities that do not perform classified research. Sarrao said that it should be acceptable for different institutions with differing risk profiles to arrive at different risk management decisions, so long as decisions are transparent.

Elabd shared that China, Russia, North Korea, and Iran were subject to intense scrutiny at A&M, but that, while country provides a starting point for analysis, specific foreign entities must also be considered. Fisher said that faculty members are encouraged to take risks, but that it is important from a scientific and international engagement perspective to have the resources that enable investigators to understand risk. He said that it is challenging when a researcher does something without understanding the risk they are taking. Additional discussion focused on the challenges universities face ensuring that faculty have risk management resources for their decision-making in potential private-sector pursuits.

6

Funding Agency Responses

Rebecca Keiser (U.S. National Science Foundation [NSF]) provided an overview of research security at NSF. She defined research security using the definition from the National Security Presidential Memorandum—33 (NSPM-33) implementation guidance:[1] "safeguarding the research enterprise against the misappropriation of research and development to the detriment of national or economic security, related violations of research integrity, and foreign government interference." Keiser noted that the definition reflects the fact that research integrity and research security are deeply intertwined. An NSF "cell diagram" of research security (see Figure 6-1) places values at the center of the cell. Keiser described the cell membrane as porous, allowing for a system that can be both open and secure.

It is crucial to interface with international partners, Keiser said, citing G7 best practices[2] indicating that openness and security are not contradictory but complementary and mutually reinforcing. Research security

---

[1] Joint Committee on the Research Environment Subcommittee on Research Security, *Guidance for Implementing National Security Presidential Memorandum 33 (NSPM-33) on National Security Strategy for United States Government-Supported Research and Development*, January 2022, p. 24.

[2] The G7 is an informal political and economic forum of seven of the world's leading economies. For G7 best practices on research security, see G7 Security and Integrity of the Global Research Ecosystem Working Group. 2024. *G7 Best Practices for Secure and Open Research*. https://science.gc.ca/site/science/en/safeguarding-your-research/general-information-research-security/international-research-security-resources/g7-best-practices-secure-and-open-research.

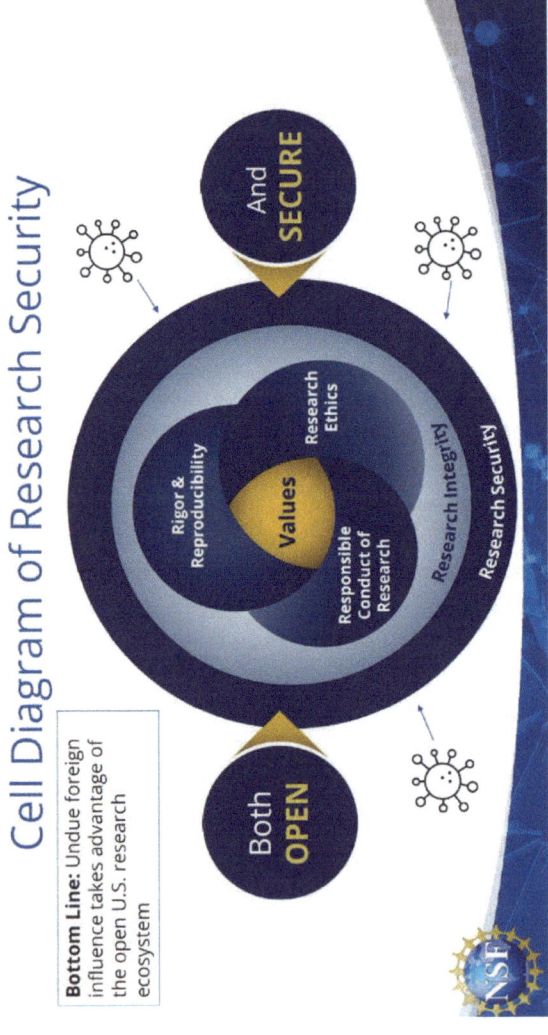

FIGURE 6-1 U.S. National Science Foundation's Cell Diagram of Research Security.
SOURCE: National Science Foundation, July 16, 2024.

needs to be considered at all stages, from fundamental research (including safeguarding researcher ideas, performing due diligence on funding sources, assessing potentially harmful end use, and differentiating international collaborations that are positive and productive from those that pose a threat to research security) to applied research (including safeguarding intellectual property, performing due diligence on sources of venture capital and investment, assessing potentially harmful end use, and vetting international transactions). Funders, research institutions, and researchers all have important roles to play in achieving research security.

Keiser highlighted NSF and other federal funding agency work:

- The White House Office of Science and Technology Policy issued guidance[3] in July on requirements for research institutions receiving $50 million or more in federal R&D funding per year over the past 3 years. The guidance states that covered research institutions must establish research security programs that include cybersecurity, foreign travel security, research security training, and export control training. Keiser emphasized that federal agencies are working together to harmonize approaches to research security.
- The NSF, National Institutes of Health (NIH), Department of Defense (DOD), and Department of Energy (DOE) co-funded the development of research security training modules. The training modules, available on NSF's website,[4] are titled as follows: What is Research Security?; Disclosure; Manage and Mitigate Risk; and International Collaboration.
- NSF is setting up the SECURE (Safeguarding the Entire Community in the U.S. Research Ecosystem) Center to serve as a clearinghouse for information to empower the research community to identify and mitigate foreign interference that poses risks to the U.S. research enterprise. The SECURE Center will share information and reports on research security risks, provide training on research security to the science and engineering community, and serve as a bridge between the research community and federal

---

[3] Office of Science and Technology Policy. 2024. *Memorandum for the Heads of Federal Research Agencies.* Guidelines for Research Security Programs at Covered Institutions, July 9, 2024. https://www.whitehouse.gov/wp-content/uploads/2024/07/OSTP-RSP-Guidelines-Memo.pdf.

[4] National Science Foundation. n.d. *Research Security Training.* https://new.nsf.gov/research-security/training.

funding agencies to strengthen cooperation on addressing research security concerns.[5]
- NSF is funding the Research on Research Security Program, which will identify and characterize attributes that distinguish research security from research integrity; improve understanding of the nature, scale, and scope of risks; provide insight into methods for identifying, mitigating, and preventing violations; and develop methodologies to assess the potential impact of threats on the U.S. economy, national security, and research enterprise.
- NSF is establishing a method for assessing research proposals for risk: TRUST (Trusted Research Using Safeguards and Transparency). The TRUST process is designed to assess whether research project personnel have active appointments or positions with entities on U.S. proscribed lists or are participating in malign foreign government talent recruitment programs. The process will also look for nondisclosure of information on appointments, activities, and sources of research support from the time after NSPM-33 implementation guidelines were released (January 2022) and will assess potential foreseeable national security applications of the research.

Harriet Kung (U.S. Department of Energy) shared the broad mission and science and technology (S&T) portfolio of DOE. The agency stewards 17 national laboratories and provides financial assistance across the full range of technology readiness levels, with awards ranging from grants to universities and loans to businesses. DOE must balance the need to protect its broad research enterprise, while promoting principled international collaborations and attracting and retaining the best and the brightest to its scientific programs. Kung displayed a timeline of research, technology, and economic security efforts at DOE (see Figure 6-2), demonstrating how DOE's approach to research security policy has evolved across multiple administrations. While working groups on research security were first formed in 2016, recent White House guidance, statutory requirements, interagency processes, and DOE's own continued evaluation of its research security policies has most recently led to the formalization of the Research, Technology, and Economic Security (RTES) Policy Working Group and the

---

[5] The SECURE Center was launched on July 24, 2024. See https://new.nsf.gov/news/nsf-backed-secure-center-will-support-research. It will be led by the University of Washington with support from nine institutions of higher education.

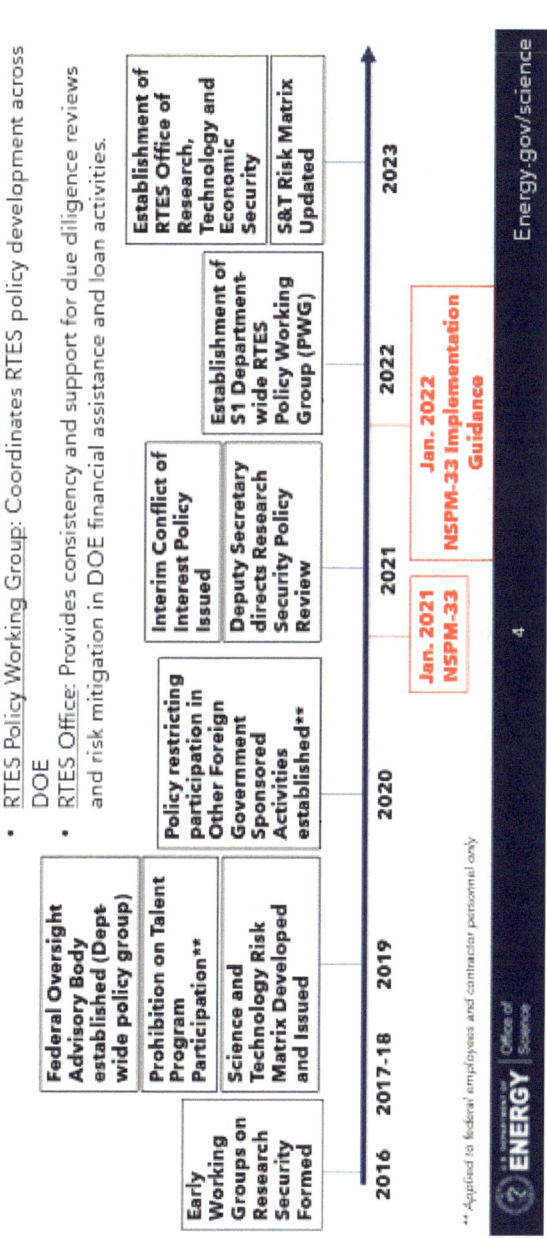

FIGURE 6-2 Evolution of research, technology, and economic security at the Department of Energy.
SOURCE: Department of Energy, July 16, 2024.

creation of the DOE RTES Office in 2023. The Office of Science works closely with the RTES Office to ensure that its due diligence reviews of research are transparent, do not create undue burden on researchers, and are risk informed by subject-matter experts. The Office of Science also participates in the annual update of the DOE S&T Risk Matrix,[6] a tool for managing risks associated with critical and emerging research and technologies activities at the national laboratories.

Kung said that engaging leaders in the scientific community is essential to building trust and creating buy-in, and results in more effective policy implementation. Close working relationships with interagency partners are equally crucial for ensuring harmonization and reducing burden on the research community. At the same time, it is essential to maintain flexibility and transparency throughout policy development.

Important questions for DOE include the following:

- How can DOE strategically balance international engagement and research security?
- As due diligence risk reviews for fundamental research are implemented, how can DOE streamline the process so as to not affect timelines for awards?
- How can DOE develop nuanced criteria for assessing research risks that recognize the (sometimes blurry) boundaries between basic, applied, and more mature stages of R&D?
- How can we transition from a compliance culture to a culture of partnership with the research community?
- How can the interagency process support program managers, principal investigators (PIs), and administrative professionals in navigating the research security landscape?

Patricia Valdez (U.S. National Institutes of Health) discussed research security efforts at NIH. In 2016, the Federal Bureau of Investigation (FBI) alerted NIH of a peer reviewer sharing confidential grant applications with overseas colleagues. The FBI also raised concerns about foreign talent recruitment programs. NIH program staff began to flag foreign affiliations used as a primary affiliation, as well as foreign grants not previously disclosed to NIH on grant applications.

---

[6] For more on the DOE's S&T Risk Matrix, see https://www.directives.doe.gov/terms_definitions/science-and-technology-risk-matrix-s-t-risk-matrix.

Since 2018, NIH has received more than 650 allegations or notifications of undisclosed research support, undisclosed employment arrangements, diversion of intellectual property, financial conflicts of interest, and conflicts of commitment where an individual has committed to full-time employment in another country while simultaneously committing to employment in the United States.[7] Valdez said that NIH works to ensure that allegations are investigated in a consistent manner.

The number of foreign interference allegations at NIH has significantly declined. In 2019, there were 184 allegations. In 2023, there were only 40. In the first part of 2024, NIH has received 11 allegations. This may be an indicator of increased awareness of research security issues, with individuals better understanding requirements and institutions more effectively communicating with researchers. Self-disclosures have increased. NIH views this as a positive because it shows that institutions are taking actions to ensure researchers follow research security procedures. Complete disclosures of the needed information in grant applications allows NIH to perform risk assessments more effectively.

In most cases, research institutions' rules apply and administrative action takes place at the institutional level. NIH administrative actions include barring an individual from performing peer review, removing an individual from a grant, and efforts to recoup funds in cases where there is conflict of commitment.

NIH works closely with other federal agencies, including those funding research, and intelligence and law enforcement agencies. Valdez notes that NIH has spent a lot of time speaking with the FBI to provide a perspective into scientists' working methods and to gain insight into intelligence and law enforcement.

Valdez said that the agency works to avoid bias or discrimination based on ethnicity when conducting investigations of research security violations. Investigations look for contradictory informa-

> "Researchers need to understand the risks that they may be taking when they enter into certain collaborations, and they should work with their institutions to mitigate the risks when possible."
> Patricia Valdez
> National Institutes of Health

---

[7] For more data on NIH foreign interference cases, see https://grants.nih.gov/sites/default/files/Foreign-Interference-6-9-24-report.pdf and https://grants.nih.gov/policy-and-compliance/policy-topics/foreign-interference/fi-data.

tion and evidence that there was an intent to deceive, and not cases of, for example, forgetting to check a box on a grant form. The People's Republic of China's talent recruitment programs explicitly target individuals of certain ethnicities. Most, but not all, NIH cases involve China, and not all cases involve scientists who are ethnically Chinese. NIH is also seeing problematic behaviors from the governments of Russia and Iran, as well as from other countries. Transparency is important, and NIH publishes procedures, data, and case studies of research security violations on their website.[8]

Valdez said that collaboration, both domestic and international, is very important to solving the most pressing and perplexing health challenges, and that the exchange of knowledge with international partners is both an essential part of innovation and crucial for our global competitiveness. But "researchers need to understand the risks they may be taking when entering into certain collaborations, and they should work with their institutions to mitigate the risks when possible." It is also important for NIH to engage with researchers to help them understand requirements and the reason for them. Valdez said that we can have robust international research collaborations and research security at the same time.

Bindu Nair (U.S. Department of Defense) said that DOD policies on research security look slightly different from other science-funding agencies' policies, but that agencies are getting to the same place. DOD began its research security efforts by examining its purpose for funding basic research. One reason is that DOD would like to support new scientific discoveries because they may result in new opportunities for meeting its mission. DOD also does not want to be surprised technologically, and if the agency does not engage in collaborative research, including with those who are not allied partners, it will not be cognizant of new ideas in S&T. DOD always wants to have the advantage of knowledge, power, tools, or technique. Finally, DOD recognizes the important role research plays in developing the workforce for the scientific enterprise of the future.

> "Same as NSF and DOE, [DOD] need[s] to have technically competent people making these highly complex, highly nuanced decisions about how to take risk. [And] we need people to be aware."
> —Bindu Nair
> Department of Defense

---

[8] See https://grants.nih.gov/policy/foreign-interference.htm.

DOD has concluded it needs to make risk-based decisions about the research it funds by using technical program staff who have a full set of information. This requires competent, technical people able to make the highly nuanced decisions about risk. PIs and institutions must be engaged in that process. Nair said that a compliance, checkbox-based approach by PIs is not going to be productive. What DOD is seeking is not a regulatory-focused approach, but a knowledge-based approach to risk assessment. DOD is in the process of aligning their policies internally across the army, navy, air force, and DARPA (Defense Advanced Research Projects Agency). However, making risk-based decisions means there will not be absolute uniformity in the way that research funding decisions are made within these agencies.

DISCUSSION

Discussion began with consideration of when risk mitigation occurs in the agency review process. Keiser said that NSF's TRUST process is being piloted on quantum technologies, and risk mitigations will be adopted after the review of projects on their scientific merit. Keiser feels strongly that input from merit review should be a factor in decisions about risk, because if a project has great merit, then a higher level of risk might be acceptable. Kung said that at DOE, the RTES Office reviews research solicitations prior to release. Once a proposal passes merit review, it may require additional review by DOE's RTES Office. Valdez said that NIH's regular risk assessments of research funding projects do not involve foreign interference reviews. Nair said that, at DOD, risk analysis happens after the selection of a proposal.

Jason Donovan (U.S. Department of State) said that he has heard concerns from European contacts about NIH's "onerous" requirements related to the review of lab notebooks. Valdez said that the policy requirement is that any domestic institution with a subaward with a foreign institution must have a policy in place stating that lab notebooks at foreign institutions are subject to review upon request. This provides a means for institutions to access these documents more easily, because in the past there have been challenges associated with securing these materials.

Moderator Michael McQuade (Carnegie Mellon University) closed the session by acknowledging hard work over the 4 years of the roundtable's existence by each of the agencies represented, in particular noting the individual efforts of Keiser, Kung, Nair, and Valdez within their agencies and in collaboration with other agencies and with stakeholders outside of government. McQuade said that collaboration both among the agencies and between the agencies and other research security stakeholders is very good.

7

Law Enforcement Agency Responses

Thomas Fingar (Stanford University) moderated a panel on the evolution of law enforcement agency responses to research security.[1] The interaction between the research community and the law enforcement and national security communities has been a centerpiece of the National Science, Technology, and Security Roundtable's (NSTSR) work. These relationships are important in order to achieve the goals of mitigating threats to U.S. national and economic security and enhancing the open and collaborative science and technology (S&T) ecosystem critical to U.S. prosperity and security. He said that, at times, the relationship has been fraught and counterproductive; however, it is now more cooperative and productive.

Fingar said that when the NSTSR was established, much of the focus was on illicit actions of foreign actors, primarily China. The China Initiative[2] was launched in 2018 as the Department of Justice's (DOJ) response to judgments that the principal threat to research security came from China and Chinese nationals. Threats were treated primarily as a law enforcement issue, and Fingar said that some actions taken by law enforcement were viewed by academic researchers as excessive, ill-founded, or harmful. Fingar added that though the China Initiative was eventually terminated, the negative effects of the initiative have lingered and the

---

[1] The Federal Bureau of Investigation was planning to participate in this panel but was unable to at the last minute due to unexpected illness.

[2] See https://www.justice.gov/archives/nsd/information-about-department-justice-s-china-initiative-and-compilation-china-related.

atmosphere it created has hindered efforts to manage the problem. During its convenings, the NSTSR was briefed on concerns from Chinese and Chinese American researchers about what seemed to be ethnic targeting by the U.S. government of Chinese and Chinese American researchers working in the United States.[3]

Charles Durant (Oak Ridge National Laboratory) said that the Department of Energy (DOE) national laboratories and the larger research community are critical to U.S. innovation and national security. He suggested that we are entering a time when the importance of national labs is growing because the United States is in nation-state competition with China, with technology as a key component. He said that the easiest way to catch up with the United States is to steal intellectual property.

In his counterintelligence work, Durant has seen theft from multiple countries. In some cases, collaborations were highly advantageous for foreign collaborators but gave little advantage to the United States. Adversaries use researchers as nontraditional collectors of information. In many cases, foreign researchers cannot decline participation in collection efforts when approached by their home country's law enforcement or internal security services. Theft also occurs through traditional covert information collection and cyber intrusions. Competitors also purchase companies to gain use of technology that was developed at national labs. One of the challenges in sharing information with the research community is that not all scientists have a security clearance, and not all are able to recognize what could be a dual-use technology.

Durant does not believe that maintaining the status quo or banning all foreign (or Chinese) researchers will solve the problem. Instead, the answer is better risk management and a better relationship between the Intelligence Community and researchers, so that trust can be established, awareness can be raised, and information can better be shared. There are many unclassified things that we can be doing research on collaboratively. However, the United States may have to identify key technologies essential to U.S. economic and national security and draw a "counterintelligence fence" around technologies that may inadvertently contribute to the development of foreign weapons or nuclear programs. The United States must have a more proactive, defensive counterintelligence program. There must

---

[3] The NSTSR was briefed on the survey of scientists of Chinese descent in the article Caught in the crossfire: Fears of Chinese-American scientists, Y. Xie, X. Lin, J. Li, Q. He, and J. Huang, *Proceedings of the National Academy of Sciences,* 120(27)e2216248120.

be a trusted security partner in the system of research who would have a security clearance and be in a position to proactively flag risks. Durant said that research security was an uphill battle 8 years ago, but that growing awareness of research security issues has made the situation better.

William Evanina (formerly of the National Counterintelligence and Security Center) discussed research security in intelligence and law enforcement agencies. He said that the United States stands out because of its research capacity and its ability to innovate and develop technology. It is a benefit to our country that talented people from around the world want to come to work in U.S. research institutions.

After the events of September 11, 2001, Evanina began working on cases of academic espionage. At that time, the threat was principally coming from three countries targeting cutting-edge university research: China, Iran, and North Korea. Two forums acted as conduits for the beneficial flow of information between federal intelligence agencies, industry, and academia: the National Security Business Alliance Council (NSBAC) and the National Security Higher Education Advisory Board (NSHEAB). The NSBAC comprised 100 industry chief executive officers with top secret clearance, who partnered with the Federal Bureau of Investigation (FBI) and Central Intelligence Agency (CIA) to share information about the techniques and tactics of corporate espionage. Separately, NSHEAB, a forum of 25 university presidents and chancellors with top secret clearance, partnered with the FBI and CIA to share information about foreign interference on campuses. NSHEAB also allowed the FBI and CIA to better understand why basic research and international collaboration is important.

> "If you look at what makes us different, it's our ability to innovate, research, [and] develop. ... Everyone who's talented around the world wants to come here."
> William Evanina
> National Counterintelligence and Security Center
> (formerly)

Evanina said that between 2013 and 2017, after NSHEAB and the NSBAC ceased to exist, dialogue between government and industry ceased. At the same time, there was an amplification of collection efforts on university campuses and a whole-of-nation approach developed by China. The U.S. government was receiving more and more leads on malign activity, such as intellectual property theft. In 2017, Evanina said that the DOJ began calling their work in this space the China Initiative because

92 percent of the investigations involved China. Around this time, the Office of Science and Technology Policy (OSTP) began engaging with the intelligence community on the issue of research security. In 2019, as director of the National Counterintelligence and Security Center, Evanina partnered with the OSTP director, Kelvin Droegemeier, to bring together the FBI and 125 university presidents and chancellors to share stories of interference on campuses. By the end of the meeting, there was agreement that action needed to be taken.

Solutions to the challenges of research security should be driven by the university community, and Evanina said that university compliance programs are key. Universities' inability to vet individuals from other countries is a challenge, and the United States has to do a better job of due diligence before we bring foreign individuals on campus.

DISCUSSION

Fingar cited both Durant and Evanina from their comments about an "increased threat," and asked how the threat is measured. Evanina responded that there is an increase in the amount of cyber and human resources China puts into these efforts. He said that China's focus is advanced manufacturing, biosciences, artificial intelligence, and quantum technologies, and that if a U.S.-based researcher is working in these areas, they will be a target of the Chinese Communist Party. China has stated this publicly. The U.S. government, Evanina said, "has to do a better job of educating and informing what the Chinese intentions are." Durant said that it is not that measures being taken by academia and others are ineffective, but that the evolving threat poses a dynamic challenge. He said that we must develop a way to share information on threats more widely in a nonclassified manner.

Fingar asked what unclassified data are available to provide an indication of the number of cases resulting in a transfer of knowledge that improved Chinese threat capacity. Durant said that it is a challenge to provide such data. He said we need to evaluate illicit theft in terms of how detrimental they are to the United States from both national and economic security perspectives. He suggested that it is more difficult to determine the effects on economic security. Evanina said that there is a significant loss each year in the United States attributable to the Chinese Communist Party and that we need platforms like NSHEAB for shared information between the intelligence and academic communities.

Maria Zuber (Massachusetts Institute of Technology) said that universities are not investigative bodies, and that they count on the federal government to vet foreign individuals wishing to come into the United States by, for example, not issuing a visa to a problematic individual. She noted that universities often receive inquiries from federal agencies for information already in the possession of other federal agencies. She agreed that there is a need for better information sharing but said that there is also a need for more clarity on the responsibilities of universities and the federal government. Evanina said that, right now, no one is vetting a scientist in China, Iran, or Russia before they apply for a job at a company or university. He said that the United States has 300,000 students every year from China, and that the State Department does not have overseas capabilities to fully investigate their backgrounds. He said that there should be a place in government that those in the private sector and universities could contact to conduct due diligence on a potential hire. Zuber said that there was discussion in the previous U.S. administration about requiring "extreme vetting" of international students. She cautioned, however, that the costs of such vetting cannot be factored into indirect cost rates. If universities had to pay that cost directly, many could not afford to hire foreign talent. Evanina said the government came close to establishing a national vetting center in 2020. Durant said that the government has very little information about foreign students. In his view, vetting is better left to universities because they have the most information about students' activities and what they have access to.

John Gannon (formerly of the National Intelligence Council) said that the climate created under the China Initiative and its assumptions, including that the researcher community was guilty of working with the Chinese government in illicit ways, led researchers to feel they were under suspicion. He posited that it was that climate, in addition to complaints that the initiative discriminated against Chinese American and Chinese-born researchers and the fact that actual prosecutions were very few, that led to the initiative's termination. Evanina suggested that the China Initiative has not been terminated. Instead, it continues to operate under a different name. He said that the number of investigative leads on foreign interference in S&T has increased 25 percent since 2020 and that there are twice as many agents and attorneys working cases now than there were in 2020. He said that the FBI does not target particular ethnicities or "go searching" for cases; rather, the FBI opens investigations on the basis of information received from universities. Gannon asked whether recent cases occurred more in universities or more in the private sector, positing that there are very few cases in universities. Evanina said that the China Initiative was about more than just academic institutions.

Durant said that national security investigations proceed at a much different pace and in a much different way than criminal investigations. In his experience, more cases are being conducted as national security investigations by intelligence professionals in an ordered process that follows the evidence. Rebecca Keiser (National Science Foundation) said that NSF continues to work closely with the DOJ on many cases, noting that, in the last several years, there have been more civil settlements than criminal prosecutions. Nevertheless, the volume of cases is very large, and she has meetings every day to discuss cases.

Jason Donovan (U.S. Department of State) referred to claims that Chinese students who receive Chinese government funding to study in the United States are obliged to report their research activities to their consulate or embassy on a regular basis. He suggested that such researchers are treated as potential targets by their home government. Evanina advocated that Chinese students have access to information from our open society so that they are not "prisoners of China while they're here in the U.S."

8

Legislative, Regulatory, and Other Types of Responses

Maria Zuber (Massachusetts Institute of Technology) moderated a panel that considered legislative, regulatory, and other types of responses to research security. Zuber said that countering the rise of China has strong bipartisan support and, while congressional actions taken on research security are generally well-meaning, actions have sometimes had deleterious effects. She said that the House Select Committee on the Strategic Competition between the United States and the Chinese Communist Party[1] has been bipartisan and thoughtful under chairs Mike Gallagher (R-WI) and John Moolenaar (R-MI). She referenced the recently issued White House Office of Science and Technology Policy guidelines for research security programs at covered institutions[2] in National Security Presidential Memorandum–33[3] (NSPM-33), noting that NSPM-33 and its implementation guidance is the result of bipartisan efforts. Zuber said that successful execution of research

---

[1] The Select Committee on the Strategic Competition between the United States and the Chinese Communist Party was formed in January 2023 in the United States House of Representatives to provide coordination regarding policy on China. See https://selectcommitteeontheccp.house.gov/.

[2] Office of Science and Technology Policy. 2024. *Memorandum for the Heads of Federal Research Agencies. Guidelines for Research Security Programs at Covered Institutions,* July 9, 2024. https://www.whitehouse.gov/wp-content/uploads/2024/07/OSTP-RSP-Guidelines-Memo.pdf.

[3] The White House. 2021. "Presidential Memorandum on United States Government-Supported Research and Development National Security Policy." National Security Presidential Memorandum–33 (NSPM-33), January 14, 2021.

security guidelines will depend on hitting the "sweet spot" between getting too prescriptive and too open-ended.

Toby Smith (Association of American Universities) identified five core principles for research security:

- Ensuring risk-based and harmonized policies across federal research agencies
- Making openness a priority to advance both science and national security
- Ensuring that research security and preserving scientific openness are complimentary, not contradictory
- Ensuring that policies avoid racial profiling and have clear mechanisms for due process
- Having researchers and universities take responsibility for assessment of risk

Smith said that there has been an "incredible" amount of work done since he began working on research security issues in 2018, referring to as examples the NSPM-33 common disclosure forms and guidelines; the creation of the National Science and Technology Council (NSTC) interagency working group; the creation of the National Science, Technology, and Security Roundtable (NSTSR); the establishment of the National Science Foundation chief research security officer, SECURE (Safeguarding the Entire Community in the U.S. Research Ecosystem) Center, and TRUST (Trusted Research Using Safeguards and Transparency) pilot program; mandatory faculty disclosure of all funding sources in research and development (R&D) award applications; and the prohibition on participation in malign foreign talent programs. While a lot has been done to address research security, it is a challenge to convince Congress that this is the case.

Smith called for the following:

1. Forum(s) like the NSTSR where stakeholders and government intelligence, security, and research officials can engage in an ongoing dialogue
2. Continued interagency collaboration, for example, the NSTC interagency working group
3. The creation of a Federal Bureau of Investigation (FBI) Liaison Office for universities at the national level

4. Better coordination among intelligence agencies in their research security efforts
5. Training for agency program officers on Controlled Unclassified Information (CUI) and controls, including when and how specific restrictions should be imposed
6. Clear processes for ensuring due process, especially in instances of agency administrative action
7. Increased sharing of information regarding clear security risks, for example, the development of mechanisms for sharing classified information with specific trusted university officials
8. Additional mechanisms to help improve research security and assess potential risks, which might, for example, employ the model of the Research and Education Networks Information Sharing and Analysis Center Cybersecurity Assessment Service[4] or involve the creation of a Federal Demonstration Partnership project related to research security and integrity
9. The development, support, and funding of new strategic international partnerships
10. Increasing retention of foreign students who graduate from American universities with advanced science, technology, engineering, and mathematics (STEM) degrees, for example, through enacting the STAPLE Act.[5]

Information designated as CUI is often sensitive personal information (e.g., student records, health information, grant proposals, and budgets), rather than national security information. Currently, there are 20 broad groupings of CUI and 120 CUI categories within those groupings,[6] and Smith said that CUI designations are challenging for program officers to understand. This, in turn, leads to a tendency to overidentify material as CUI, which triggers a set of requirements from the federal government that are "tough and expensive."

In responding to the challenges of research security, Smith said that it is important to avoid requiring excessive and duplicative reporting by faculty and/or institutions; developing lists of "sensitive research" for which faculty would be unable to share and publish their scientific results; overly

---

[4] See https://www.ren-isac.net/services/pas/index.html.
[5] H.R. 2717, 115th Congress (2017–2018). See https://www.congress.gov/bill/115th-congress/house-bill/2717/all-info.
[6] See https://www.archives.gov/cui/registry/category-list.

restricting the ability of U.S. researchers to participate in important international scientific partnerships; adding new categories of CUI; making significant changes to how we treat fundamental research for purposes of export control; and reinstating the China Initiative.

Smith said that scientific progress requires science to be open and replicable, testable, and reproducible. It is important to consider the costs versus benefits of closed versus open science, and they must not be viewed as mutually exclusive. The United States no longer has a monopoly on the top science. National security requires investments in fundamental scientific research and not merely walling it off. National security also requires the development of a national talent recruitment, retention, and development strategy. Universities and government must work together to ensure research security, research integrity, and continued scientific openness.

> "National security requires the development of a national talent recruitment, retention, and development strategy."
> Toby Smith
> Association of American Universities

Paul Doucette (Batelle) said that Batelle has a significant role in a number of federally funded research and development centers (FFRDCs), including eight Department of Energy national labs. DOE has had protections in place to shield research ever since the Manhattan Project, but such measures are unprecedented for civilian science agencies. He suggested that intelligence personnel who understand the importance of managing risk and the need to preserve openness and collaboration while simultaneously protecting research and intellectual property are missing from the conversations about research security. For FFRDCs, there has been a pivot from thinking about export controls and dual-use technologies in the context of national security to thinking about economic security as well.

DOE is a member of the Intelligence Community and is the largest federal sponsor of open, collaborative, basic research in the physical sciences. This fact is part of what has drawn additional scrutiny to DOE in recent years. Being a member of the Intelligence Community means that DOE labs have access to threat assessments and information, which are valuable and informative. But it also means that DOE and its national labs fall under the jurisdiction of the House and Senate Intelligence Committees, which, together with the House and Senate Armed Services Committees, has put the agency under increased scrutiny, especially regarding concerns about China. There has also been scrutiny from the committees with programmatic jurisdiction over DOE and the House Select Committee on the Strategic Competition between the United States and the Chinese Communist Party.

The House and Senate National Defense Authorization Acts for Fiscal Year 2025 both have provisions that would prohibit access to DOE labs by certain foreign nationals.[7] This is problematic because open, collaborative research is crucial to the national labs' work on nuclear deterrents. An open research environment also provides encouragement for the best and brightest scientists from around the world to work at our national labs. DOE has controls and infrastructure in place to manage risks from foreign entities and measures to advance open collaborative research while also protecting intellectual property. DOE performs extensive screening of anyone who accesses laboratories or laboratory networks and has security measures in place to limit access of foreign nationals who come on to their sites. The department rejects about 10 percent of foreign national requests to access DOE sites.

Doucette enumerated policy principles and recommendations in the categories of transparency, consistency, balance, encouraging innovation, and resourcing appropriately. For increased transparency, he recommended updating systems to enable better tracking and sharing of information and improving data quality and reliability. For improving consistency, he recommended developing common definitions and standardized policies and procedures, while acknowledging differences among DOE's national labs. To achieve balance in policies, he recommended prioritizing risk management rather than attempting risk avoidance, as well as balancing the protection of research and intellectual property with open collaboration in order to advance science. He recommended encouraging innovation by sharing best practices among national laboratories, universities, and federal agencies. Finally, he emphasized the importance of appropriately resourcing not only research security and counterintelligence efforts but also R&D programs. Doucette concluded by saying that "the best defense is a good offense."

DISCUSSION

Richard Meserve (formerly of the Carnegie Institution), advocated for aggressive limits on the use of the CUI designation, calling for an exam-

---

[7] The provisions that prohibit access to DOE labs by certain foreign nationals in the House and Senate versions of the 2025 National Defense Authorization Act are:
House: H.R. 8070 § 3111
Senate: S.4638 § 3120

ination of CUI and greatly reducing the number of categories. Smith said that CUI categories have become a "catchall for everything" and that there should be more training, suggesting that not all CUI categories should be treated equally. He suggested there should be training for program officers about changing the designation of research from fundamental to protected research, including when such changes should take place. John Gannon (formerly of the National Intelligence Council) expressed agreement for Smith's recommendation to establish an FBI Liaison Office for universities at the national level but said that providing federal resources for such an office would be an issue.

Smith said that both Republicans and Democrats agree it is necessary to create an immigration pathway for highly skilled STEM talent; however, in the current polarized political environment, immigration reform is a fraught topic. As a result, reforms to highly skilled STEM immigration policies will not be addressed until comprehensive immigration reform is achieved.

Michael McQuade (Carnegie Mellon University) said that it would be beneficial for cleared university presidents and vice presidents of research (and perhaps compliance officers) to have a venue to be able to discuss threats. It is important to establish a flow of information to aid decision-making within universities. Given evidence of the threats to research security, McQuade now assumes a zero-trust environment for foreign engagement. We need to think, he said, about what would define demonstrable trust among allies and partners rather than focusing so much on China. Doucette said that in some cases, countries the United States considers allies are also countries we need to be careful about collaborating with. Just because someone is an ally does not mean we can trust them in international collaborations. Rather, it is about managing risk for collaborating with all international partners. Smith said that today's ally might be tomorrow's adversary.

9

Potential Near- and Long-Term Responses on Research Security

Kathryn A. Moler (Stanford University) moderated the workshop's final panel, a session that considered future responses for meeting the goal of securing scientific research while preserving openness in the research system of the United States. Moler began the session by summarizing key themes from the preceding workshop sessions: the importance of providing appropriate resources for both addressing research security and maintaining U.S. research preeminence; the need to properly assess and categorize research that needs protection; the importance of expertise to support being able to make security decisions case by case; the need for a strong talent development program within the United States; thinking about talent as a supply chain issue; the importance of shared values in conducting research; and the appropriate response in instances where shared values are not present.

Kelvin Droegemeier (University of Illinois Urbana-Champaign), former director of the White House Office of Science and Technology Policy, said that there has been a lot of progress on research security over the last several years, commending the National Science, Technology, and Security Roundtable (NSTSR) and its communications efforts.

Droegemeier said that U.S. global competitiveness is proportional to our capabilities and investments, and inversely proportional to threats to (and interference with) our values. We should "lead with our values," which are the principles by which we operate. Values must not be compromised, as they constitute a necessary and an inseparable dimension of research. These values can be returned to when disagreement or confusion arises. For the United States, national and research values include honesty, integrity, transparency, accountability, openness, collaboration, fairness, merit-based competition, objectivity, and reciprocity (see Figure 9-1). The United States can live up to our values by strengthening and actively promoting messaging on our values and holding continuous conversation on values to deepen cultural norms; linking values to research security measures and open science; and highlighting values as a benefit to performing research in the United States and in international collaborations.

Droegemeier said that we should "not play to not lose." The United States has taken a much more defensive position that stems, in part, from intentional efforts by adversaries to force the United States to expend resources on the challenges of research security. We must also "untie our hands" by reducing regulations. Currently, nearly 50 percent of researcher time is spent on administrative activities. The Office of Management and Budget and its Office of Information and Regulatory Affairs should work with nongovernmental organizations such as the Council on Government Relations, Association of American Universities, Association of Public and Land-grant Universities, and Federal Demonstration Partnership to identify specific research regulations and policies that can be changed or suspended under executive order to reduce administrative burdens on researchers.

Droegemeier said that it is critical that the United States invest in talent development on a national level and cited as precedent for this the G.I. Bill (P.L. 78-346), National Defense Education Act of 1958 (NDEA; P.L. 85-864), and Post 9/11 Veterans Educational Assistance Act of 2008 (P.L. 110-252). In addition, the United States must look beyond the visible horizon and develop a comprehensive, multisector, whole-of-nation, 25-year science and technology (S&T) vision for the country. There are inherent challenges to this, for example: the United States' decentralized, multisector structure challenges planning and coordination; responsibility for agency budgets and priorities are spread across Congress; and interagency collaboration often depends on intangibles (e.g., the personalities involved or who is working to make things happen). However, short-term thinking is no longer a viable option.

Droegemeier called upon the National Academies of Sciences, Engineering, and Medicine to take a leadership role in crafting a national S&T security strategy. It is challenging for the executive branch, the White House, Congress, a laboratory, a university, or a university consortium to lead on this. The National Academies is in the best position to lead this

Our National and Research Values

- Honesty
- Integrity
- Transparency
- Accountability
- Openness
- Freedom of inquiry
- Sharing
- Collaboration
- Merit-based competition
- Mutual respect
- Fairness
- Impartiality
- Inclusivity
- Objectivity
- Civil debate
- Reciprocity
- Principled international collaboration
- Other…

FIGURE 9-1 U.S. national research values.
SOURCE: Kelvin Droegemeier, July 17, 2024.

effort because it is viewed as having effective convening ability and a neutral status. It would be important to have co-chairs who are stakeholders to help gain buy-in from affected communities.

Diana Gehlhaus (Special Competitive Studies Project) spoke about growing and cultivating the U.S. science, technology, engineering, and mathematics (STEM) workforce. Leaks in the talent pipeline occur consistently throughout the pipeline, starting at kindergarten and continuing through the college years. Less than one-third (28 percent) of STEM-educated workers are working in a STEM job. The number of STEM degrees awarded in the United States is rising, but the number of STEM degrees awarded in China is rising at a greater pace (see Figure 9-2). Gehlhaus said that "foreign-born talent is the backbone of America's innovation power," but there is increased competition for talent. China has had talent programs for many years, and there is evidence that these programs have been effective.[1] Without the right climate, policies, and infrastructure, there is no guarantee that foreign-born talent educated in the United States will want to stay, especially as China continues to invest in its innovation ecosystem and infrastructure. The United States is already losing top artificial intelligence researchers, 59 percent and 11 percent of whom were located in the United States and China, respectively, in 2019. In 2022, those numbers were 42 percent in the United States and 28 percent in China.

Gehlhaus said that the National Defense Education Act of 1958 was a "game changer" for education policy in the United States and called for an "NDEA 2.0." Gehlhaus considers the CHIPS and Science Act (P.L. 117-167) to be a recent iteration of NDEA, as well as certain National Science Foundation initiatives. The key is to understand what combination of skills and competencies will be needed for the United States to maintain its competitive edge.

On research security, the Special Competitive Studies Project recommends taking a risk-based approach to decisions on whether international individuals should be allowed to work in the United States. Also, that it is possible to impose risk-based decisions that protect U.S. intellectual property without limiting needed inflows of talent. The project recommends denying visas to those with identified high-risk factors, regularly evaluating research security policy through an interagency process, and staying up to

---

[1] Gehlhaus provided the following evidence that China's talent programs have been effective: D. Shi, W. Liu, and Y. Wang. *Has China's Young Thousand Talents Program been Successful in recruiting and Nurturing Top Chinese Scientists?* July 2022. https://papers.ssrn.com/sol3/papers.cfm?abstract_id=4043516.

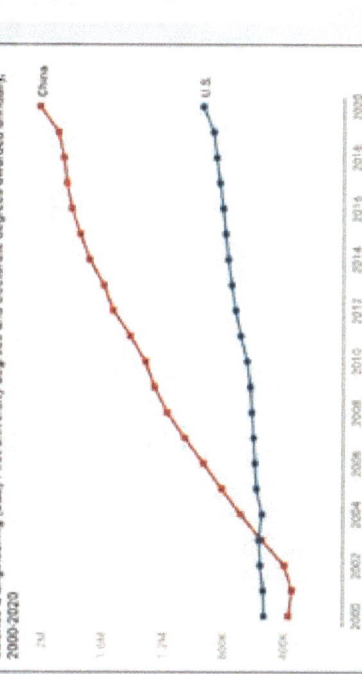

FIGURE 9-2 STEM degrees in the United States versus China.
SOURCE: Diana Gehlhaus, July 17, 2024.

date on trends in emerging and dual-use technologies so that decisions are technology informed.

The Special Competitive Studies Project also makes recommendations for increasing workforce competitiveness: making classrooms artificial intelligence–enabled by 2030, cultivating an advanced industry workforce, achieving high-skilled immigration reform by raising visa caps and reforming green card quotas, and creating a National Commission on Artificial Intelligence and the Future of Work that would champion consensus-based reform.

Norbert Holtkamp (Hoover Institution) discussed his June 2024 paper, co-authored with NSTSR members Thomas Mason and Anna Puglisi, "How to Create, and Sustain, R&D Leadership: A Blueprint for International Collaboration."[2] The premise of the paper is that an open and inclusive research system provides the fastest way to progress new discoveries and maintain our leadership. There is no doubt that the open, collaborative scientific environment has been compromised, there are threats faced by the United States, and we must act. However, because of U.S. response to these threats, funding organizations, universities, national labs, and principal investigators (PIs) spend significant time implementing risk-mitigating measures, assessing these measures, and training staff. This, in turn, has led to delays in achieving the primary objective of research: moving fast scientifically and staying ahead. Such delays allow our adversaries to catch up with us even faster. Enacting risk-mitigating measures also costs money, which diverts valuable research dollars away from performing research.

> "Working with like-minded countries can protect our respective innovation bases, by developing an international agreement—including verification mechanisms—that would enable free collaborations while guarding against the actions of nations that do not adhere to those norms."
> Norbert Holtkamp
> Hoover Institution

Enacting the recommendations of the most recent JASON report to review every proposal and understand every risk, Holtkamp said, will be

---

[2] The paper is available at https://www.hoover.org/research/how-create-and-sustain-rd-leadership.

cumbersome. Further, achieving perfect security is not possible, so either way there will be risk.

Holtkamp said that these problems around science and security are not new and have been solved in other areas, for example, nuclear non-proliferation agreements. Such agreements allow for regulations to take place at a national level, rather than at an individual, university, or national lab level. Countries agree to the rules of the agreement and receive advantages in the form of access to technology and expertise.

To solve the challenges of research security, Holtkamp suggested that the United States assemble allies and partners with common values, write them down, and agree to abide by those values and the principles of international collaboration (and agree on an enforcement mechanism). A streamlined, risk-managed process among member countries, their institutions, and PIs would provide a kind of "TSA Pre-Check" lane for approval of international research collaborations. The incentive to stay in the agreement would be the ability to participate in international exchange and access to infrastructure, researchers, and data. Holtkamp said that such an arrangement would restore an open and fast research ecosystem and provide for an attractive work environment for the best and brightest from anywhere in the world.

Moler ended the panel presentations by sharing thoughts from absent NSTSR member Thomas Mason (Los Alamos National Laboratory). Mason, she said, strongly supports the "TSA Pre-Check" idea that Holtkamp presented and believes that when advancing U.S. S&T, "it's all about the offense."

DISCUSSION

Rebecca Keiser (U.S. National Science Foundation) said that conversations about a trusted international research network have taken place in international forums. When asked about levers available to reach privately funded researchers or other non-federally funded researchers, Holtkamp said that privately funded researchers would be affected to a lesser degree by the plan, but that it would allow publicly funded researchers to return to a mode in working with friendly countries that they are used to. Holtkamp's co-author, Anna Puglisi, said that it would be possible to broaden the "TSA Pre-Check" idea to all sectors of U.S. S&T, but the paper represented an effort to lay out steps to begin to scope the idea, starting with the question: How do you enhance collaboration? By values, norms, standards? The authors felt it was important to make the answers to these questions explicit, because so much is assumed about international collaboration.

John Gannon (formerly of the National Intelligence Council) expressed support for Droegemeier's call for a national S&T security strategy, asking who might lead this effort. Droegemeier reiterated that the National Academies could convene a multisector, nationwide, politically independent effort. Droegemeier said that such a strategy "shouldn't look like anything we've done before, because if it does, it isn't going to be helpful."

10

Possible Future Directions for Securing Scientific Research While Preserving Openness in the U.S. Research System

To conclude the workshop, National Science, Technology, and Security Roundtable (NSTSR) members each had an opportunity to provide thoughts on the roundtable's 4 years of work looking at U.S. national science, technology, and security.

Rebecca Keiser (U.S. National Science Foundation) lauded the role the NSTSR played in productively convening academia, intelligence, and federal science agencies, and said that discussions among these communities must continue with the goal of acting on the problem. Communication across these communities has improved over the past 4 years, and the research community now more widely acknowledges security concerns raised by intelligence and law enforcement agencies. Keiser prefers the phrase "risk management" rather than "risk avoidance," and we should encourage international collaboration with the goal of managing risk rather than avoiding risk. The science and technology (S&T) community is still unclear about what is, and what is not, allowable in international collaboration, and we must get to a point where researchers are able to feel confident collaborating internationally. She appreciated NSTSR members' acknowledgment that the U.S. government is being proactive and has made many good steps forward on addressing the challenges of research security.

Thomas Fingar (Stanford University) said that many of the problems that imperil U.S. S&T preeminence (such as adequate STEM education at the secondary level, counterproductive immigration policies, inadequate research funding, and cumbersome regulations) were created by U.S. policy and are within our control to fix. External threats from bad actors provide additional challenges. Over the past 4 years, dialogue, best practices sharing, education, and attention to the problem have improved the situation. However, to understand what the appropriate remedies are, we must better understand the scale of the problem of theft of research in the university sector. The problem in the private sector is larger in magnitude than in the university sector, Fingar said. The China Initiative leaves a challenging legacy, and there must be regular dialogue and mutual education between universities and law enforcement agencies. While China makes more of an effort to exploit the open U.S. S&T system than other countries, it is not the only country that does so, and excessive focus on China risks losses from our research system to other countries.

Anna Puglisi (Hoover Institution) said that the United States must cultivate a robust S&T system by building an innovation base, developing talent, maintaining big science facilities, and sustaining research funding over time. Puglisi said that having extreme policy reactions, such as closing our doors to China or doing nothing, will impede our ability to compete and will ultimately benefit China. We cannot treat China like any other country because of its policies to crack down on civil society, restrict access to academic publications, and remove academic freedom language from university charters. She said that most U.S. policy actions to date have been tactical and not designed to counter the Chinese system of government, which is inherently different from our own, threatens academic freedom, and manipulates public opinion. Chinese scientists, businesspeople, officials interacting with universities, companies, and research entities must respond to the Chinese government and security services if they are asked for information. China is increasingly intimidating and harshly silencing its critics, including Chinese citizens abroad and U.S. citizens. Because of this, we cannot forget what is at stake.

Jason Donovan (U.S. Department of State) said that the United States must be clear-eyed on the risk posed by China, while we adhere to our values and apply them in a nation-agnostic way when making decisions on trusted international scientific collaborations. The Department of State is working to build international consensus around research security, and there is broad agreement among partners and allies on what values are important for conducting research amongst democratic societies. However, countries have very different science ecosystems and hence divergent policy levers that can be used to influence federally funded research. This makes it difficult to envision a singular global regime which could certify the integrity of all international research collaboration. The Department of State is introducing research security language in international S&T agreements—including on researcher protections, intellectual property, and data reciprocity—and is focusing international agreements more deliberately on achieving mutual benefit. Speaking personally, Donovan stressed the importance of exercising humility, given that the United States does not always live up to the values we seek to promote internationally, and Donovan believes we must rededicate ourselves to presenting a more compelling vision, calling for a "purposeful dedication of our country's efforts and resources to solving meaningful challenges that are uplifting for us as a people."

Bindu Nair (U.S. Department of Defense) said that we must enhance the U.S. fundamental research enterprise, but that it is also critical to translate fundamental scientific research into applications. Such translation is a part of an offensive strategy for competing with our adversaries; however, we do not have sufficient understanding of how to do it effectively. The United States must also harness more research talent, including by attracting more talent from other countries, improving our domestic education system, and providing good projects for students and researchers to work on. Nair identified topics for further research: better understanding of innovation in a nondemocratic society and better understanding of who wins in a system of open scientific research.

Chaouki Abdallah (Georgia Institute of Technology) underscored an assertion made earlier in the workshop by Kelvin Droegemeier: that China is playing to win, and the United States is playing not to lose. He said that China is becoming more confident, and the United States is becoming less so. China exploited the vulnerabilities of the U.S. open scientific system, and one way to counter that is to double down on our strength: our values. We can also counter China's malign activities by increasing trade with other countries, including by leveraging American soft power. Researchers are being asked to report on international relationships and agreements from 2010, but this is not useful because it was before the China Initiative was instituted. The world has changed, and we must look forward to win this competition, not backward.

Michael McQuade (Carnegie Mellon University) said that societal well-being is inextricably linked to U.S. national and economic security and that the U.S. innovation ecosystem is a tremendous national asset that must be protected. He said the United States must adopt a risk-based approach to decisions about international collaborations by identifying risks, assessing their probability, and analyzing what consequences would result. Negative outcomes that might result from such collaborations must be included in the analysis of consequences. However, positive outcomes that might be precluded by blocking the collaboration must also be included in the analysis. The United States must diversify our international talent pool, as it is not good practice to so extensively concentrate our source of international STEM (science, technology, engineering, and mathematics) talent in China. Moving forward, the United States must have venues to share expert information on security threats in the S&T ecosystem and must bring the private sector into this dialogue more.

John Gannon (formerly of the National Intelligence Council) said that effective risk management should be prioritized as one of the more urgent issues facing us in the challenge of research security. Security and science stakeholders must work together to implement U.S. policies in an atmosphere of good faith negotiation directed both at containing a real and growing foreign threat and at protecting U.S. research as a vital national security asset. Science and security must partner in a more productive way to share knowledge about the U.S. innovation ecosystem and about the foreign threat to it. Policies must be implemented effectively, which is a challenge in a complicated S&T ecosystem and a complex government. The National Academies of Sciences, Engineering, and Medicine should ensure that the observations and insights learned in the work of the NSTSR are disseminated to the larger community, and this effort must be properly resourced and staffed.

Maria Zuber (Massachusetts Institute of Technology) said that the amount of U.S. federal funding for research is in decline, an important context to U.S. global competitiveness and the NSTSR's focus on federal research funding. In addition to foreign interference in federally funded scientific research, nonfederal research must also be examined. There must be improved engagement between the academic research community and the Federal Bureau of Investigation (FBI). The academic research community must engage with the FBI according to the FBI's practices as a security agency, and not expect that the FBI will operate according to the open standards and norms of academia. Helpful actions could be taken by Congress on research security, but not all proposed legislation is helpful. It will require efforts by the research community to advocate for productive policies. Restrictions placed on research collaborations should be based on the risk of the proposed collaboration, not merely based on the technology involved. Talent is the greatest supply chain challenge in the United States, and we will not continue to be a world leader without it.

Richard Meserve (formerly of the Carnegie Institution) focused his comments on what remains to be done to address research security challenges. The application of Controlled Unclassified Information restrictions needs to be evaluated so that they are not applied excessively. The private sector composes a large part of the U.S. innovation ecosystem, but the scale of S&T theft by foreign countries in the private sector is not well understood. U.S. statutes relating to research security identify the need to protect both national and economic security; however, it is not clear what is meant by economic security separate from national security, and how economic security relates to research security. There is a need for an adequately staffed and resourced forum to provide opportunities for further interaction among communities with a stake in research security.

11

Concluding Session: A Brief Summary and Synthesis of the Capstone Workshop

At the end of the workshop, planning committee chair Kathryn A. Moler (Stanford University) presented a summary and synthesis of the workshop themes with a slide presentation that she had prepared during the 2 days as speakers presented. She provided a brief summary of each speaker's comments, as well as suggestions of potential actors to be assigned to each of the recommendations provided by Toby Smith in the session "Legislative, Regulatory, and Other Types of Responses," drawn from sidebar discussions during the workshop. (See the link in Appendix D for Moler's slides.)

Moler suggested that we must gather more data to better understand the problem of research security, including the percentage of open research collaborations with scientists from the People's Republic of China that result in ethical violations.

Appendix A

Abbreviated Agendas for NSTSR Regional Meetings

Mid-Atlantic Regional Meeting
University of Maryland
March 31, 2023

Welcome
    Gregory Ball, Vice President for Research, University of Maryland, College Park and University of Maryland, Baltimore

Addressing the Need to Protect Research in the University Environment
    Catherine Johnson, Republican Staff Director, Research and Technology Subcommittee, House Science, Space, and Technology Committee
    Dahlia Sokolov, Democratic Staff Director, House Science, Space, and Technology Committee

Addressing Faculty Fears and Concerns About Research Security Initiatives
    Christine Ciocca Eller, Former Co-Chair, National Science and Technology Council Subcommittee on Research Security

Fostering and Maintaining Meaningful Partnerships with Domestic Security and Intelligence Services
    Susan Thompson, Federal Bureau of Investigation
    John Hartnett, Federal Bureau of Investigation

Issues in National Academies' Research Security Activities
    Sarah Rovito, National Academies of Sciences, Engineering, and Medicine

Overview of the National Science Foundation's Research Security and Integrity Information Sharing and Analysis Organization
    Rebecca Keiser, Chief of Research Security Strategy and Policy, National Science Foundation

Overview of the Group of Seven's (G7) Virtual Academy
    Patricia Valdez, Chief Extramural Research Integrity Officer, Office of Extramural Research, National Institutes of Health

APPENDIX A

New England Regional Meeting
Massachusetts Institute of Technology
May 22, 2023

Discussion with Industry Representatives
    Dean Geribo, Head of Corporate Security, Moderna
    Nikki Rutman, Director of Global Intelligence, Moderna
    Maggie Buck, Threat Management, Moderna
    Danielle Holland, Senior Vice President, General Counsel and Corporate Secretary, AVEO
    Kevin Swindon, Corporate Vice President for Global Security, Charles River

The Massachusetts Institute of Technology (MIT) China Report
    Richard Lester, Co-Chair, MIT China Report, Associate Provost for International Activities and Japan Steel Industry Professor of Nuclear Science and Engineering
    Lily Tsai, Co-Chair, MIT China Report, Chair of the Faculty, Ford Professor of Political Science, Director of the MIT Gov/Lab
    Suzanne Berger, John M. Deutch Institute Professor and Professor of Political Science
    Peter Fisher, Thomas A Frank Professor of Physics, Director of the MIT Office of Research Computing and Data
    M. Taylor Fravel, Arthur and Ruth Sloan Professor of Political Science, Director of the Security Studies Program
    David Goldston, Director, MIT Washington Office
    Yasheng Huang, Epoch Foundation Professor of International Management, Director of Action Learning at MIT Sloan School of Management
    Daniela Rus, Andrew and Erna Viterbi Professor of Electrical Engineering and Computer Science, Director of the Computer Science and Artificial Intelligence Laboratory
    Elizabeth Dupuy, Senior Advisor, Office of the Associate Provost for International Activities, Staff to the MIT China Strategy Group

International Research Collaborations at Boston University
    Kate Mellouk, Associate Vice President for Research Compliance
    Kevin Gallagher, Director, Boston University Global Development Policy Center, Professor of Global Development Policy

Emerging Technologies and Research Security
    David Cox, IBM Director of the MIT-IBM Watson Artificial
        Intelligence Laboratory

APPENDIX A 77

Midwest Regional Meeting
Northwestern University
October 11-12, 2023

Welcome
    Michael H. Schill, President, Northwestern University

Pressures Chinese Students Face from the Chinese Government While Studying at American Universities
    Yaqiu Wang, Research Director for China, Hong Kong and Taiwan, Freedom House

An FBI Field Office Case Study
    Special Agent Jonathan Willett, Federal Bureau of Investigation, Little Rock Field Office

Federal Funding Agency Research Security Panel
    Kristopher Gardner, Director for Science and Technology Protection, Office of the Under Secretary of Defense for Research and Engineering, Department of Defense
    Rebecca Keiser, Chief of Research Security Strategy and Policy, National Science Foundation

Central Midwest Research Security Forum Panel
    Holly Bante, Associate Vice President for Research Security and Ethics, University of Cincinnati
    Elizabeth Wagner, Senior Director of Research Security and Export Controls, Purdue University
    Lisa Nichols, Executive Director of Research Security, University of Michigan
    Amy Weber, Senior Director of Export Control and International Compliance, Northwestern University

Vice Presidents for Research Panel
    Jacqueline Jeruss, Associate Vice President for Research Integrity and Compliance, University of Michigan
    Susan Martinis, Vice Chancellor for Research and Innovation, University of Illinois Urbana-Champaign

Eric Perreault, Vic President for Research, Northwestern University
Jeff Rhoads, Vice President for Research, University of Notre Dame

Research Security at Manufacturing USA Institutes
Federico Sciammarella, Chief Technology Officer, MxD (Manufacturing x Digital)
John Wilzynski, Executive Director, America Makes

Research Security at Department of Energy Laboratories
Paul Kearns, Director, Argonne National Laboratory
Brian Sherin, Senior Advisor, Fermi National Accelerator Laboratory

APPENDIX A

Pacific Regional Meeting
The Hoover Institution at Stanford University
January 23-24, 2024

Welcome and Introductory Remarks
    Condoleezza Rice, Tad and Dianne Taube Director, Hoover Institution

Welcome
    Richard Saller, President, Stanford University

Federal Funding Agency Perspectives on Research Security
    Rebecca Keiser, Chief of Research Security Strategy and Policy, National Science Foundation
    Harriet Kung, Deputy Director for Science Programs, Office of Science, Department of Energy
    Michael Lauer, Deputy Director for Extramural Research, National Institutes of Health
    Bindu Nair, Director for Basic Research, Department of Defense

Research Security in the University of California System
    Alex Bustamante, Senior Vice President, Chief Compliance and Audit Office, University of California

Perspectives on Research Security from Academic Researchers in the Pacific Region
    Bruce DeBruhl, Associate Professor, Computer Science and Software Engineering, California Polytechnic State University, San Luis Obispo
    Christopher J. Keane, Vice President for Research, Washington State University
    Edl Schamiloglu, Distinguished Professor, Department of Electrical and Computer Engineering, University of New Mexico

The U.S. Scientific Enterprise and Nations of Concern
    Siegfried S. Hecker, Senior Fellow, Freeman Spogli Institute for International Studies; Emeritus and Research Professor, Management Science and Engineering, Emeritus, Stanford University

Michael McFaul, Director, Freeman Spogli Institute for International Studies; Ken Olivier and Angela Nomellini Professor of International Studies, Department of Political Science, Stanford University; Peter and Helen Bing Senior Fellow, Hoover Institution

Larry Diamond, Mosbacher Senior Fellow of Global Democracy, Freeman Spogli Institute for International Studies; Senior Fellow, Hoover Institution; and Professor, by courtesy, of Sociology and of Political Science, Stanford University

Abbas Milani, Hamid and Christina Moghadam Director of Iranian Studies, Stanford University; Professory, by courtesy, Stanford Global Studies Division

Enhancing Collaboration in Science and Security
Nicholas Shenkin, Federal Bureau Special Agent; National Security Affairs Fellow, Hoover Institution

Research Security and Biotechnology
Carol Burns, Deputy Director for Research and Chief Research Officer, Lawrence Berkeley National Laboratory
Drew Endy, Martin Family University Fellow in Undergraduate Education; Senior Fellow, by courtesy, Freeman Spogli Institute; Senior Fellow, by courtesy, Hoover Institution; Faculty Co-Director of Degree Programs, Hass Plattner Institute of Design, Stanford University
Aine Hanly, Executive Vice President and Chief Technology Officer, Vir Biotechnology
Steve Laderman, Director, Agilent Research Laboratories

Research Security and Computer Science
Bill Dally, Chief Scientist and Senior Vice President, NVIDIA
Dave Orr, Director of Engineering for AI Safety and Alignment, Google DeepMind
William A. Pike, Chief Science and Technology Officer, National Security Directorate, Pacific Northwest National Laboratory
Katherine Yelick, Robert S. Pepper Distinguished Professor of Electrical Engineering and Computer Sciences and Vice President for Research, University of California, Berkeley

Research Security and Aerospace
- Sigrid Elschot, Associate Professor of Aeronautics and Astronautics and, by courtesy, of Electrical Engineering, Stanford University
- Larry D. James, Deputy Director, Jet Propulsion Laboratory, California Institute of Technology
- Alison Nordt, Director for Space Science and Instrumentation, Advanced Technology Center, Lockheed Martin

Southern Regional Meeting
Texas A&M University
March 7, 2024

Welcome
    Susan Ballabina, Chief of Staff, Texas A&M University President Jack Welsh

Federal Funding Agency Perspectives on Research Security
    Rebecca Keiser, Chief of Research Security Strategy and Policy, National Science Foundation
    Harriet Kung, Deputy Director for Science Programs, Office of Science, Department of Energy
    Patricia Valdez, Chief Extramural Research Integrity Officer, Office of Extramural Research, National Institutes of Health
    Bindu Nair, Director for Basic Research, Department of Defense

International Perspectives on Research Security
    Jung-Kyu Jung, Director of R&D Asset Protection Team, Korea Institute of S&T Evaluation and Planning, Republic of Korea
    Kit Hardman, Research Collaboration Advice Team, Department for Science, Innovation, and Technology, United Kingdom
    Mirko van Muijen, International Cooperation Director, European Commission
    Shawn McGuirk, Deputy Director of Research Security, Natural Sciences and Engineering Research Council, Canada

Perspectives from Vice Presidents of Research
    Majed Dweik, Vice President of Research and Economic Development, Alabama A&M University
    Giovanni Piedimonte, Vice President for Research, Tulane University
    Magesh Rajan, Vice President for Research and Innovation, Prairie View A&M University

Research Security and Agricultural Research and Technology
    Chris Holly, Partner, Cooley
    Mahendra Bhandari, Assistant Professor, Digital Agriculture, Texas A&M University

Gregory Pompelli, Director, Center of Excellence for Cross-Border Threat Screening and Supply Chain Defense, Texas A&M University

Sonny Ramaswamy, President, Northwest Commission on Colleges and Universities; former Director, National Institute of Food and Agriculture

Appendix B

Workshop Agenda

**National Science, Technology, and Security Roundtable
Capstone Workshop**

July 16–17, 2024
Keck Center of the National Academies
500 5th Street, NW
Washington, DC 20001
Room 101

AGENDA

Tuesday, July 16

10:00 am*   Welcome, Meeting Overview

10:10 am   The Work of the National Science, Technology, and Security Roundtable (NSTSR)

           NSTSR Co-Chairs:
           John Gannon, Former Chairman, National Intelligence Council (retired)
           Richard Meserve, President Emeritus, Carnegie Institution

Maria Zuber, E. A. Griswold Professor of Geophysics, Massachusetts Institute of Technology

10:40 am   Discussion

11:00 am   The U.S. Research System's Role in National and Economic Security

Rapporteur:
Michael McQuade, Special Advisor to the President, Carnegie Mellon University

Speakers:
Patrick Gallagher, Professor of Physics, University of Pittsburgh
Susan Gordon, Former Principal Deputy Director of National Intelligence

11:30 am   Discussion

12:00 pm   Lunch Break

12:45 pm   Evolution of University and National Lab Responses

Rapporteur:
Chaouki Abdallah, Executive Vice President for Research and Professor of Electrical and Computer Engineering, Georgia Institute of Technology (virtual)

Speakers:
Joe Elabd, Vice Chancellor for Research, Texas A&M University System
Peter Fisher, Thomas A. Frank Professor of Physics, Massachusetts Institute of Technology (virtual)
John Sarrao, Director, SLAC National Accelerator Laboratory

1:30 pm   Discussion

APPENDIX B   87

2:00 pm   Evolution of Funding Agency Responses

            Speakers:
            Rebecca Keiser, Chief of Research Security Strategy and
                Policy, National Science Foundation
            Harriet Kung, Acting Director, Office of Science,
                Department of Energy
            Bindu Nair, Director for Basic Research, Department of
                Defense
            Patricia Valdez, Extramural Research Integrity Officer,
                Office of Extramural Research, National Institutes of
                Health

2:45 pm   Discussion

3:15 pm   Break

3:45 pm   Evolution of Law Enforcement Agency Responses

            Rapporteur:
            Thomas Fingar, Shorenstein APARC Distinguished Fellow,
                Freeman Spogli Institute for International Studies,
                Stanford University

            Speakers:
            Charles Durant, Field Intelligence Element Director,
                Oak Ridge National Laboratory (virtual)
            William Evanina, Former Director, National
                Counterintelligence and Security Center

4:30 pm   Discussion

5:00 pm   Wrap-Up of Day One and Preview of Day Two

5:15 pm   Adjourn Day One

Wednesday, July 17

10:00 am	Welcome, Recap of Day One, and Overview of Day Two
10:10 am	The Nature of the Geopolitical Challenge

Rapporteur:
Anna Puglisi, Hoover Institution

10:25 pm   Discussion

10:40 am   Legislative, Regulatory, and Other Types of Responses

Rapporteur:
Maria Zuber, E. A. Griswold Professor of Geophysics, Massachusetts Institute of Technology

Speakers:
Paul Doucette, Vice President of Government Relations and Public Policy, Batelle
Toby Smith, Vice President for Policy, Association of American Universities

11:25 am   Discussion

11:55 am   Lunch Break

12:30 pm   Potential Near- and Long-Term Responses

Rapporteur:
Kathryn Moler, Chodorow Professor of Applied Physics, Physics, and Energy, Stanford University

Speakers:
Kelvin Droegemeier, Professor of Atmospheric Science and Special Advisor to the Chancellor for Science and Policy, University of Illinois
Diana Gehlhaus, Director for Economy, Special Competitive Studies Project

APPENDIX B

                Norbert Holtkamp, Science Fellow, Hoover Institution, and Professor of Particle and Particle Astrophysics and Photon Science, SLAC National Accelerator Laboratory

1:30 pm   Discussion

2:00 pm   Possible Future Directions, Including Ideas for Further Research

                Members of the National Science, Technology, and Security Roundtable

3:15 pm   Brief Summary and Synthesis of the Capstone Workshop

                Kathryn Moler, Chodorow Professor of Applied Physics, Physics, and Energy, Stanford University

3:30 pm   Adjourn Workshop

*All Times Eastern Daylight Time

Appendix C

Workshop Advance Reading Materials

1. Paper by National Science, Technology, and Security Roundtable Co-Chairs John C. Gannon, Richard A. Meserve, and Maria T. Zuber. See Appendix F.
2. National Science, Technology, and Security Roundtable of the National Academies of Sciences, Engineering, and Medicine. Meeting Agendas: 2020–2024. https://www.dropbox.com/home/NSTSR%20Capstone%20Workshop%20July%2016-17%2C%202024/NSTSR%20Meeting%20Agendas%202020-2024.
3. Anna Puglisi. 2003. Testimony before the Senate Committee on Energy and Natural Resources on "recent advances in artificial intelligence and the Department of Energy's role in ensuring U.S. competitiveness and security in emerging technologies," September 7, 2003. https://www.energy.senate.gov/services/files/28466A9C-08EE-4E6D-A58B-197907A05F92.
4. Norbert Holtkamp, Thomas Mason, and Anna Puglisi. 2024. "How to Create, and Sustain, R&D Leadership." Hoover Institution, June 3, 2024. https://www.hoover.org/research/how-create-and-sustain-rd-leadership.
5. National Academies of Sciences, Engineering, and Medicine. 2022. *Protecting U.S. Technological Advantage.* Washington, DC: The National Academies Press. https://doi.org/10.17226/26647. https://nap.nationalacademies.org/catalog/26647/protecting-us-technological-advantage.

Appendix D

Workshop Slide Presentations

1. Rebecca Spyke Keiser (Chief of Research Security Strategy and Policy [CRSSP], National Science Foundation), *Overview of Research Security.*
   https://www.nationalacademies.org/documents/embed/link/LF2255DA3DD1C41C0A42D3BEF0989ACAECE3053A6A9B/file/D7E9AAD9C0FF93B7822A5E9E4344C706762B505BD62B?noSaveAs=1.

2. Harriet Kung (Acting Director, Office of Science, U.S. Department of Energy), *Evolution of DOE Responses.*
   https://www.nationalacademies.org/documents/embed/link/LF2255DA3DD1C41C0A42D3BEF0989ACAECE3053A6A9B/file/DDAA19AA1A14B0F0F4DCB67FC3143338742FD1EB5640?noSaveAs=1.

3. Paul Doucette (Vice President of Government Relations and Public Policy, Battelle), *Legislative, Regulatory & Other Responses to Ensure Research Security, Integrity, & Scientific Progress.*
   https://www.nationalacademies.org/documents/embed/link/LF2255DA3DD1C41C0A42D3BEF0989ACAECE3053A6A9B/file/D6AB1F849E569A512902220D1B5F50831C0BC98F8B67?noSaveAs=1.

4. Toby Smith (Vice President for Policy, Association of American Universities), *Legislative, Regulatory & Other Responses to Ensure Research Security, Integrity & Scientific Progress.*

https://www.nationalacademies.org/documents/embed/link/
LF2255DA3DD1C41C0A42D3BEF0989ACAECE3053A6A9B/
file/D02B6FFA020284FB902AA2E7016A6EAEFDAD4E8
BD559?noSaveAs=1.

5. Kelvin K. Droegemeier (Professor of Atmospheric Science and Special Advisor to the Chancellor for Science and Policy at the University of Illinois Urbana-Champaign), *Potential Near- and Long-Term Responses*.
https://www.nationalacademies.org/documents/embed/link/
LF2255DA3DD1C41C0A42D3BEF0989ACAECE3053A6A9B/
file/D3B327BA685D865E85A94C11772C9823D5C04
B7821B0?noSaveAs=1.

6. Diana Gehlhaus (Director for Economy, Special Competitive Studies Project), *Untitled*.
https://www.nationalacademies.org/documents/embed/link/
LF2255DA3DD1C41C0A42D3BEF0989ACAECE3053A6A9B/
file/D54B8DBB6D0CC8DCD819206B5D959ED0CE02
F85D30AB?noSaveAs=1.

7. Norbert Holtkamp (Science Fellow, Hoover Institution), *A Possible Future Direction*.
https://www.nationalacademies.org/documents/embed/link/
LF2255DA3DD1C41C0A42D3BEF0989ACAECE3053A6A9B/
file/D70B69E504C4B0184835621663BE26002331888
EA650?noSaveAs=1.

8. Kathryn Moler (Marvin Chodorow Professor and Professor of Applied Physics, of Physics and of Energy Science Engineering, Stanford University), *Brief Summary and Synthesis*.
https://www.nationalacademies.org/documents/embed/link/
LF2255DA3DD1C41C0A42D3BEF0989ACAECE3053A6A9B/
file/D478C85C43AD256B824B2107DC844365C415DE9
F497A?noSaveAs=1.

Appendix E

Biographical Sketches of Workshop Participants

Chaouki T. Abdallah*[1] joined the Georgia Institute of Technology on September 1, 2018, as a professor of electrical and computer engineering and the executive vice president for research. Prior to that, he was a professor of electrical and computer engineering (ECE) at the University of New Mexico (UNM). He also served as chair of the ECE department at UNM between 2005 and 2011, and as provost of UNM between July 2011 and August 2018. Between January 2017 and February 2018, he also served as the 22nd president of UNM. As the chief research officer of Georgia Tech, Abdallah provides overall leadership for the institute's $1 billion portfolio of research, economic development, and sponsored activities, including the Georgia Tech Research Institute, 11 interdisciplinary research institutes, and related research administrative support units. He also serves on the executive committee of the Council on Research for the Association of Public and Land-grant Universities, the executive committee for the National Academies of Sciences, Engineering, and Medicine's Government-University-Industry Research Roundtable, and the advisory committee for the Center for Measuring University Performance. Abdallah obtained his bachelor of engineering degree from Youngstown State University in 1981, and his M.S. and Ph.D. in electrical engineering from Georgia Tech in 1982 and 1988, respectively. Abdallah conducts research and teaches

---

[1] An asterisk (*) indicates a member of the National Science, Technology, and Security Roundtable.

courses in the general area of systems theory with focus on control, communications, and computing systems. Abdallah is a senior member of the Institute of Electrical and Electronics Engineers (IEEE), is a recipient of the IEEE Millennium medal, and is fluent in English, French, and Arabic.

Jason Donovan* is a career member of the U.S. Senior Foreign Service, class of Counselor. He joined the service in 1999, after working in academia and in the private sector as a technology entrepreneur. He served his first tours in Guatemala and Italy, prior to returning to Washington, D.C., where he worked in the State Department's Operations Center and on the Executive Secretariat staff. Donovan coordinated regional security initiatives in Southeast Asia before moving to the U.S. Embassy in New Delhi, where he worked as the deputy in the Economic Section focusing on clean energy cooperation. After being recalled to Washington to serve as director for South Asia at the National Security Council, he was State Department deputy director for Western Europe, then director for multilateral and global affairs. Donovan led the International Narcotics and Law Enforcement section at the U.S. Mission in Pakistan before joining the U.S. Embassy in London as political counselor. He assumed his duties as director of the Office of Science and Technology Cooperation in September 2022. He speaks French, Spanish, and Italian.

Paul Doucette is vice president of government relations and public policy at Battelle, the world's largest nonprofit research and development organization. In addition to managing Battelle's government relations team and overseeing the operation of the Battelle Washington Office, he is responsible for issues related to the Department of Energy's Office of Science and National Nuclear Security Administration and advises corporate leadership and the directors of the Battelle-affiliated national laboratories on relevant policy and budget matters. Before joining Battelle in 2008, Doucette was legislative director and science and technology advisor to U.S. Representative Judy Biggert (R-IL), a senior member of the House Science and Technology Committee, former chairman of its Energy Subcommittee during the 108th and 109th Congresses, and co-founder of the House Research and Development Caucus. In this capacity, he worked closely with senior scientists and management at Argonne National Laboratory—located in Biggert's district—to identify and advance the laboratory's legislative priorities. He joined Representative Biggert's staff in 1999 after serving as a legislative aide in the Washington, D.C. office of Illinois Governor

Jim Edgar, where he was responsible for state-federal relations on energy and environmental issues. Originally from Rochester, Minnesota, and now residing in Alexandria, Virginia, he received a B.S. in business and public administration in 1997 from Drake University, and now serves on its Board of Trustees.

Kelvin Droegemeier is professor of atmospheric science and special advisor to the chancellor for science and policy at the University of Illinois Urbana-Champaign. Droegemeier served as the Regent's Professor of Meteorology, Weathernews Chair Emeritus, and Roger and Sherry Teigen Presidential Professor at the University of Oklahoma, where he had been a member of the faculty from 1985 to 2023. He previously served as the University of Oklahoma's vice president for research from 2009 to 2018 and founded and served for 5 years as director of the Sasaki Institute, which fostered the development and application of knowledge, policy, and advanced technology for societal impact. He served as chair of the Association of Public and Land-grant University's Council on Research Policy and Graduate Education (now the Council on Research) and is a fellow of both the American Meteorological Society and the American Association for the Advancement of Science (AAAS). Droegemeier's federal science and policy leadership roles include serving on the National Science Board from 2004 to 2016, the last 4 years as vice chair, and directing the White House Office of Science and Technology Policy (OSTP) from 2019 to 2021. Concurrent with his leadership of OSTP he also served as acting director of the National Science Foundation for two and a half months in 2020. At the state level, he was appointed to the Oklahoma Governor's Science and Technology Council, serving from 2011 to 2019, and as cabinet secretary of science and technology from 2017 to 2019.

Charles Durant began his professional career in national intelligence in 1980 when he joined the U.S. Army as a German-language signals intelligence voice interceptor, and he served military tours at U.S. Army Field Station Berlin in West Berlin; Fort Huachuca, Arizona; Fort Meade, Maryland; and Fort Carson, Colorado. After the fall of the Berlin Wall, Durant transitioned to U.S. Army Counterintelligence in 1993 and served tours at the BENELUX (Belgium, Netherlands, Luxembourg) Military Intelligence Detachment, the 10th Special Forces Group at Fort Carson, and the U.S. Army Foreign Counterintelligence Activity (USAFCA) at Fort Meade as well as a deployment to Hungary in support of the international peacekeeping mission in the former Yugoslavia. Durant retired from the army in 2000 and returned to USAFCA as a counterintelligence agent. After 9/11, he went to work for the National Security Agency until he returned to USAFCA as the chief of investigations. He then served as U.S. Army representative to the Department of Defense Counterintelligence Field Activity before assuming a position with the White House Military Office, where he provided counterintelligence and security support to the President and White House staff on overseas visits. In 2009, he joined the Department of Energy (DOE) Office of Intelligence and Counterintelligence. In 2011, he became the DOE deputy director of counterintelligence until his retirement from federal service as a member of the Senior Executive Service. After his retirement from federal service in April 2019, Durant worked as the Berkshire Hathaway Energy director of national security and resiliency policy in Washington, D.C. In October 2020, he joined Oak Ridge National Laboratory as field intelligence element director and conducts frequent external engagement with sponsors across the U.S. Intelligence Community. He has more than 43 years of intelligence community experience and in 2019 was recognized for his service by the DOE secretary of energy with a Meritorious Service Award, the National Nuclear Security Administrator's Distinguished Service Gold Award, and a Lifetime Counterintelligence Achievement Award by the director of National Intelligence's National Counterintelligence and Security Center.

Joe A. Elabd is a vice chancellor for research at the Texas A&M University System, a system of 11 universities and 8 state agencies with externally funded research expenditures of $1.3 billion annually. As the leader of the A&M System Office of Research, Elabd provides research leadership and services to support all 19 system members and oversees numerous offices and initiatives, including Texas A&M Innovation, National Laboratories Office, Bush Combat Development Complex, Texas A&M Semiconductor Institute, Texas A&M Fort Worth, Research Security Office, Research Compliance Office, Research Administration Office, Research Development Office, and the Chancellor's Research Initiative. Prior to these roles, Elabd served in several administrative roles at Texas A&M University, including the interim vice chancellor and dean of engineering, interim director of the Texas A&M Engineering Experiment Station, associate dean for research of engineering, and associate department head of chemical engineering. Elabd is also currently a professor and the Axalta Coating Systems Chair II in the Artie McFerrin Department of Chemical Engineering at Texas A&M

University. He is a fellow of the American Physical Society and served as a senior fellow at the Instituto di Studi Avanzati, Università di Bologna, and a scholar in residence at the Food and Drug Administration. He has received numerous research awards including the National Science Foundation CAREER Award, the Army Research Office Young Investigator Award, and the DuPont Science and Engineering Award. His research focuses on electrochemical energy (batteries, capacitors, fuel cells) and materials and polymer science. Elabd has taught chemical engineering courses at all levels (freshmen, sophomore, junior, senior, and graduate). He received his Ph.D. and B.S. in chemical engineering from Johns Hopkins University and University of Maryland, Baltimore County, respectively, and was a National Research Council postdoctoral fellow at the U.S. Army Research Laboratory.

William Evanina was confirmed by the U.S. Senate on May 6, 2020, to be the first Senate-confirmed director of the National Counterintelligence and Security Center (NCSC). Evanina served as the director of NCSC from June 2, 2014, to January 20, 2021. In this position, he was the head of Counterintelligence (CI) for the U.S. government. Evanina was responsible for leading and supporting the CI and security activities of the U.S. Intelligence Community, the U.S. government, and U.S. private-sector entities at risk from intelligence collection or attack by foreign adversaries. Under NCSC, he oversaw national-level programs and activities such as the National Insider Threat Task Force; personnel security and background investigations; information technology protection standards and compliance; CI cyber operations; supply chain risk management; threat awareness to sectors of the U.S. critical infrastructure; and national-level damage assessments from espionage or unauthorized disclosures, CI mission management, and national CI and security training programs. Under Evanina's leadership, NCSC produced the President's *National Counterintelligence Strategy of the United States of America 2020*, which has been instrumental in raising foreign intelligence threat awareness to critical infrastructure sectors and private-sector executives regarding supply chain, economic security, cyber, and malign foreign influence. Evanina chaired the National Counterintelligence Policy Board and the Allied Security and Counterintelligence Forum, which comprised senior CI and security leaders from Australia, Canada, New Zealand, and the United Kingdom. Evanina also served as chair of the NATO Counterintelligence Panel. Prior to his selection as the director of NCSC, Evanina served as the chief of the Central Intelligence Agency's Counterespionage Group. He previously served as assistant special agent in charge of the FBI's Washington Field Office, where he led operations in both the Counterintelligence and Counterterrorism Divisions. He served more than 31 years of distinguished federal service, 24 of which as a special agent with the FBI. At the start of his law enforcement career in 1996, he investigated organized crime and violent crimes through the FBI's Newark Field Office. He then served on an FBI SWAT unit for 10 years, ultimately supervising this unit. He led some of the highest profile terrorism investigations in our nation's history, including the 9/11 attacks, the anthrax attacks, and the Daniel Pearl kidnapping. During his tenure with the FBI's Joint Terrorism Task Force, Evanina was selected as a supervisory special agent and received the FBI Director's Award for Excellence for his leadership in the investigation into convicted spy Leandro Aragoncillo. Evanina's government career began in 1989 as a project manager with the General Services Administration in Philadelphia. He holds a bachelor's degree in public administration from Wilkes University in Wilkes Barre, Pennsylvania, and a master's degree in educational leadership from Arcadia University in Philadelphia. He currently serves as founder and CEO of the Evanina Group advising CEOs and boards of directors on strategic corporate risk.

Thomas Fingar* is the Shorenstein Asia-Pacific Research Distinguished Fellow in the Freeman Spogli Institute for International Studies, Stanford University. From 2005 through 2008, he served as deputy director of national intelligence for analysis and, concurrently, as chairman of the National Intelligence Council. Fingar served previously as assistant secretary of the U.S. State Department's Bureau of Intelligence and Research (2000–2001 and 2004–2005), principal deputy assistant secretary (2001–2003), deputy assistant secretary for analysis (1994–2000), director of the Office of Analysis for East Asia and the Pacific (1989–1994), and chief of the China Division (1986–1989). Between 1975 and 1986, he held various positions at Stanford University, including senior research associate in the Center for International Security and Arms Control. Fingar is a graduate of Cornell University, with an A.B. in government and history, 1968, and Stanford University, with an M.A., 1969, and Ph.D., 1977, in political science.

Peter Fisher is an American experimental particle physicist, as well as the Thomas A. Frank (1977) Professor of Physics and the former head of the Department of Physics of the Massachusetts Institute of Technology (MIT). He is a fellow of the American Physical Society. From 1989 to

1994, Fisher was on the faculty of Johns Hopkins University. He joined the MIT faculty in 1989 and became a full professor in 2001. His research has included 12 years at CERN (European Organization for Nuclear Research) working on the Alpha Magnetic Spectrometer for the International Space Station. His research interests also include the detection of dark matter, development of new particle detectors, compact energy supplies, and wireless energy transmission. He released his first book in 2022, *What is Dark Matter?*, synthesizing his own and peers' research on the topic. He was chair of the MIT Department of Physics from 2014 to 2022. He became the first head of the MIT Office of Research Computing and Data in 2022. He is a member of JASON (advisory group). Fisher became a fellow of the American Physical Society in 2006. He was named a fellow for the American Association for the Advancement of Science in 2020. He earned a B.S. in engineering physics at the University of California, Berkeley, in 1983, and a Ph.D. in nuclear physics at the California Institute of Technology in 1988.

Patrick Gallagher is a professor of physics at the University of Pittsburgh, following 9 years as chancellor (2014–2023). Prior to joining Pitt, Gallagher served for 21 years at the National Institute of Standards and Technology (NIST), in various roles, including as director of the NIST Center for Neutron Research between 2004 and 2008, and as NIST director and undersecretary of commerce for standards and technology between 2009 and 2014. Between 2013 and 2014 he was concurrently acting as deputy secretary of commerce. Gallagher has served on many independent boards, including for the Association of American Universities, the Association of Public and Land-grant Universities, and Internet2. He has also served on the National Commission on Forensic Science (co-chair, 2014) and the National Commission on Enhancing Cybersecurity (2014). He has a doctorate in physics from the University of Pittsburgh. He has previously served on several National Academies boards and committees, including as co-chair of the Committee on Protecting Critical Technologies for National Security in an Era of Openness and Competition, as a member of the Committee for an Assessment of and Outlook for New Materials Synthesis and Crystal Growth, and on the Board on Physics and Astronomy (2007–2009) and the Neutrino Facilities Assessment Committee (2002–2003).

John C. Gannon* is the former chairman of the National Intelligence Council. He is currently an adjunct professor in the graduate Security Studies Program at Georgetown University. He served in numerous positions at the Central Intelligence Agency, including as director of European analysis, as deputy director for intelligence, assistant director of central intelligence for analysis and production, and as chairman of the National Intelligence Council. After his retirement from the Central Intelligence Agency in 2001, he served in the White House as the head of the intelligence team standing up the Department of Homeland Security and later as the staff director of the U.S. House Select Committee on Homeland Security. He retired from the UK-owned BAE Systems in 2012 as president of the $1.7-billion Intelligence and Security Sector, which supported intelligence, defense, and homeland-security missions. From 2014 to 2015, he was the executive director of the congressionally directed 9/11 Review Commission of the FBI. He earned his B.A. in psychology at Holy Cross College, and his M.A. and Ph.D. in history at Washington University in St. Louis. Gannon is a member of the Council on Foreign Relations and the Board of Directors of Voices of September 11th. He has served on numerous committees of the National Academies.

Diana Gehlhaus is the director for economy at the Special Competitive Studies Project. She was a research fellow at the Center for Security and Emerging Technology (CSET) and the senior advisor for talent in the Chief Digital and Artificial Intelligence Office at the U.S. Department of Defense under an Interdepartmental Personnel Act agreement with CSET. Previously, she was a doctoral fellow at the RAND Corporation, receiving her Ph.D. in policy analysis from the Pardee RAND Graduate School. Gehlhaus's research focuses on the intersection of technology and talent, including domestic talent pipelines in artificial intelligence and other emerging technologies; workforce development and education policy; youth career and educational decision-making; trends in employer hiring, recruiting, and retention; military and federal civilian talent management; and technology and telecommunications policy. Prior to RAND she was an economist and director of the Young American Prosperity Project at the Progressive Policy Institute, a policy analyst at the U.S. Export-Import Bank, and an economist for the Bureau of Labor Statistics. She has an M.A. in applied economics from Johns Hopkins University and a B.A. in mathematics and economics from Bucknell University. Her media appearances include CNBC, Comcast Newsmakers, Wisconsin Public Radio, Nevada Public Radio, and the Richard Fowler Show. Her research and commentary have been featured in *The Hill*, *USA Today*, *Fortune*, *The Washington Post*, and the *Harvard Business Review* blog, among other outlets.

Susan Gordon is the former principal deputy director of national intelligence, serving from 2017 to 2019, where she advised the President on intelligence matters and provided operational leadership of the agencies and organizations of the Intelligence Community (IC). She is a widely respected authority on risk management, technical innovation, and cyber and space issues. She is an active board member and university fellow, and advises private companies in the areas of technology, strategy, and leadership. Throughout Gordon's more than three decades in the IC, she led large-scale organizational change and delivered revolutionary outcomes. She worked to adapt the IC to emerging economic, military, and political trends affecting the current operating environment. Gordon led the establishment of In-Q-Tel, the Central Intelligence Agency's venture capital arm, in the 1990s. In the last several years, she has focused on advancing intelligence integration across the IC, expanding outreach and partnerships to the private sector and international allies, and driving innovation across the IC. While serving as deputy director of the National Geospatial-Intelligence Agency (NGA) from 2015 to 2017, Gordon helped lead NGA through a transformation to adapt to emergent challenges. In this role, she spearheaded agile decision-making, modernization of the information environment, and the expansion of geospatial intelligence services to the open marketplace. She joined the Central Intelligence Agency in 1980 and served for 29 years, rising to senior executive positions in each of the agency's four directorates: operations, analysis, science and technology, and support. Gordon holds a bachelor of science from Duke University.

Norbert Holtkamp has a joint appointment at Stanford University as both a science fellow at the Hoover Institution and professor of particle and particle astrophysics and photon science at SLAC National Accelerator Laboratory. He provides support in growing SLAC's portfolio with the Department of Energy and the private sector and focuses on what the future of international science collaborations could look like as part of the Technology, Economics and Governance Working Group at the Hoover Institution. He was SLAC's deputy laboratory director from 2014 to 2022 and led the conception and implementation of the multi-laboratory partnerships of several DOE and DOE/National Science Foundation projects. Since 2019 he has also led SLAC's $1.1 billion LCLS-II Free Electron Laser construction project, built by five U.S. national laboratories, which transitioned to operation in September 2023. He managed the laboratories' overall risk portfolio, which included more than $2.5 billion worth of construction on the SLAC site. When joining SLAC in November of 2010 he began as the associate laboratory director for the Accelerator Directorate. In 2006, he was nominated principal deputy director of the ITER organization. ITER, an international organization in the South of France, includes seven members: EURATOM as part of the European Commission, China, India, Japan, Korea, Russia, and the United States, and comprises a construction project worth more than 20 billion Euro. From 2001 to 2006, he served as the director of the Accelerator Systems Division for the $1.4 billion Spallation Neutron Source at Oak Ridge National Laboratory, which still is the world's most powerful pulsed neutron source built by a collaboration of six DOE national laboratories. He held various leadership positions on a variety of U.S. and international science infrastructure projects at Fermi National Accelerator Laboratory in Chicago, Illinois, and DESY in Hamburg, Germany. He has an M.S.-equivalent degree in physics from the University of Berlin and a Ph.D. in physics from the Technical University in Darmstadt, Germany. His interests include science applications, technology transfer, and the value and future of international science collaborations. In June 2008, he received the Gersh Budker Prize of the European Physical Society.

Rebecca Spyke Keiser* is chief of research security strategy and policy (CRSSP) at the National Science Foundation (NSF). She has served as head of the Office of International Science and Engineering since 2015. The office promotes an integrated, international strategy and manages internally focused programs that are innovative, catalytic, and responsive to a broad range of NSF and national interests. Keiser is the first CRSSP, a position established in March 2020 to ensure the security of federally funded research while maintaining open international collaboration. In this role, Keiser provides the NSF director with policy advice on all aspects of research security strategy. She also leads NSF's efforts to develop and implement efforts to improve research security and the agency's coordination with other federal agencies and the White House. She has a bachelor's degree in Japanese studies from Wellesley College, a master's degree in politics of the world economy from the London School of Economics, and a doctorate in international studies from the University of South Carolina.

Harriet Kung* is the acting director of the Office of Science at the U.S. Department of Energy. She was previously deputy director for science programs, and in that role was the senior career official providing scientific and management direction and oversight for the Office of Science research programs, including Advanced Scientific Computing Research, Basic Energy Sciences, Biological and Environmental Research, Fusion Energy Sciences, High Energy Physics, and Nuclear Physics, as well as other supporting functions and offices. Kung served in various leadership roles in Basic Energy Sciences, the largest program in the Office of Science, from 2002 to 2020. Before joining DOE in 2002, Kung was a technical staff member and a project leader at Los Alamos National Laboratory. Her research focused primarily on nanoscale materials and high-temperature superconductivity. With more than 20 years of service in DOE, she led and cultivated one of the nation's premier physical sciences programs. During her tenure, she developed a new basic research paradigm in team-science approach to advance DOE's science and energy missions by spearheading a decade-long strategic planning initiative to assure timely, science-based solutions. She also positioned the Office of Science as a National Quantum Initiative leader by establishing strategies to capitalize on strong synergy between disciplines such as physics, biology, materials, and engineering, as well as the world-leading scientific user facilities. She has chaired and co-chaired high-level interagency working groups to develop and implement national science priorities. Kung received her M.S. and Ph.D. degrees from Cornell University. She is the recipient of numerous awards, including the Presidential Meritorious Executive Rank Award in 2009 and the Distinguished Executive Rank Award in 2022.

Thomas E. "Thom" Mason* has served as the director of Los Alamos National Laboratory since November 2018. Previously, he was the senior vice president for Global Laboratory Operations at Battelle, where he had responsibility for governance and strategy across the six National Laboratories that Battelle manages or co-manages. Prior to joining Battelle, he worked at Oak Ridge National Laboratory (ORNL) for 19 years, including 10 years as the laboratory director. Under his leadership, ORNL saw significant growth in programs, new facilities, and hiring while achieving record low safety incident rates. Before becoming laboratory director, he was associate laboratory director (ALD) for Neutron Sciences, ALD for the Spallation Neutron Source, and director of the Experimental Facilities Division. During his time in Oak Ridge, Mason was active in the community serving as chair of the Oak Ridge Public Schools Education Foundation as well as Innovation Valley, the Knoxville–Oak Ridge area regional economic development organization. He moved to ORNL from the University of Toronto, where he was a faculty member in the Department of Physics and previously worked as a senior scientist at Risø National Laboratory and a postdoc at AT&T Bell Laboratories. For the past 30 years, he has been involved in the design and construction of scientific instrumentation and facilities and the application of nuclear, computing, and materials sciences to solve important challenges in energy and national security. Mason has a Ph.D. in experimental condensed matter physics from McMaster University and a B.Sc. in physics from Dalhousie University.

J. Michael McQuade* is special advisor to the president of Carnegie Mellon University, and previously served as vice president for research, providing leadership for the university's research enterprise and advocating for the role that science, technology, and innovation play nationally and globally. From 2006 to 2018 he served as senior vice president for science and technology at United Technologies Corporation, where he provided strategic oversight and guidance for research, engineering, and development activities that focused on a broad range of high-technology products and services for the global aerospace and building systems industries. McQuade held senior positions with technology development and business oversight at 3M, Imation, and Eastman Kodak. He served as vice president of 3M's Medical Division and president of Eastman Kodak's Health Imaging Business. He has broad experience managing basic technology development and the conversion of early-stage research into business growth. He holds Ph.D., M.S., and B.S. degrees in physics from Carnegie Mellon University. He served as a member of the President's Council of Advisors on Science and Technology and of the Secretary of Energy Advisory Board and is a member of the Defense Innovation Board.

Richard A. Meserve* is president emeritus of the Carnegie Institution for Science. He is also senior of counsel at the law firm Covington & Burling LLP. Before assuming the Carnegie presidency in April 2003, he was chairman of the U.S. Nuclear Regulatory Commission, having served since October 1999. He currently serves as chairman of the International Nuclear Safety Group, chartered by the International Atomic Energy Agency. Early in his career, he served as legal counsel to the President's science advisor and law clerk to Justice Harry A. Blackmun of the United States Supreme Court and to Judge Benjamin Kaplan of the Massachusetts Supreme Judicial Court. Meserve received a B.A. from Tufts University, a J.D. from Harvard Law School, and a Ph.D. in applied physics from Stanford University. He is a member of the National Academy of Engineering and has previously served on numerous committees and boards of the National Academies.

Kathryn A. Moler* is the Marvin Chodorow Professor and professor of applied physics, physics, and energy sciences and engineering at Stanford University. She conducts research in magnetic imaging, develops tools that measure nanoscale magnetic fields, and studies quantum materials and devices. Among other honors, she received a national Presidential Early Career Award for Scientists and Engineers, held a Packard Fellowship for Science and Engineering, received the William L. McMillan Award "for her fundamental studies of the superconducting pairing state, Josephson vortices, and the role of interlayer coupling in high-temperature superconductors," and was elected a fellow of the American Physical Society. To honor her sustained commitment to teaching, the American Association of Physics Teachers awarded her the Richtmyer Award for Outstanding Leadership in Physics Education, and Stanford appointed her as the Sapp Family Fellow in Undergraduate Education. She was previously the senior associate dean of natural sciences in the School of Humanities and Sciences and the director of the Stanford Nano Shared Facilities. She is a member of the NanoFront (TU-Delft/Leiden) Scientific Advisory Board and the Physics Frontier Center—Joint Quantum Institute Advisory Board.

Bindu Nair* is director for basic research at the U.S. Department of Defense, within the Office of the Secretary of Defense (OSD). In this role, she is responsible for oversight and coordination of the department's $2.2 billion investment in basic science. This investment supports high-risk and high-payoff basic research projects in physical science, life science, environmental science, applied mathematics, and other fields that probe the limits of today's technologies and discover new phenomena and know-how that may ultimately lead to future technologies for the DOD. Prior to her assignment to OSD, Nair worked for the Department of the Army with oversight responsibilities for the science and technology program in power and energy. She has worked in the DOD laboratory system at Natick Soldier Research, Development and Engineering Center as well as in private industry at Foster Miller (Waltham, Massachusetts). Her research expertise is in the field of material science and engineering including nanomaterials, polymers, and organic electronic materials, and she has taught graduate level courses in polymer synthesis. She has published primarily in membrane and materials development fields and holds patents in fuel cell technologies. Nair holds a B.Sc. from the University of Florida and a Ph.D. from the Massachusetts Institute of Technology in materials science and engineering.

Anna Puglisi* is currently the CEO and founder of a boutique consulting firm that helps governments, companies, and research entities secure their technology and personnel. She also serves as a senior advisor to the National Security Commission on Emerging Biotechnology. Previously she was an adjunct professor at Georgetown University and a senior fellow at Georgetown's Center for Security and Emerging Technology, where she focused on science and technology (S&T) policy development and global technology competition, and was the national counterintelligence officer for East Asia, advising senior U.S. and foreign government officials at the highest levels, academia, and the private sector on counterintelligence issues including research security. She has played a prominent role in drafting U.S. national S&T strategies and in designing mitigation strategies for both the public and private sectors to protect technology. She has received numerous awards including the FBI Director's Award for Excellence. Puglisi holds an M.P.A., an M.S. in environmental science, and a B.A. in biology with honors, all from Indiana University. She studied at the Princeton in Beijing Chinese language school and was a visiting scholar in Nankai University's Department of Economics, where she studied China's S&T policies, infrastructure development, and university reforms. She is a co-author of the 2013 study *Chinese Industrial Espionage*, the first book-length treatment of the topic, as well as countless related proprietary studies. She is proficient in Mandarin Chinese.

John Sarrao became SLAC National Accelerator Laboratory's sixth director in October 2023. He came to SLAC from Los Alamos National Laboratory (LANL) in New Mexico, where he served as the deputy director for science, technology, and engineering. In that role he led multiple directorates, including chemistry, earth and life sciences, global security, physical sciences, and simulation and computation. He also stewarded technology transitions and served as LANL's chief research officer in support of its national security mission. Before becoming deputy director, he also served as associate director for theory, simulation, and computation and division leader for materials physics and applications at LANL. Sarrao's scientific research focus is superconductivity in materials. He studies the synthesis and characterization of correlated electron systems, especially actinide materials. He won the 2013 Department of Energy's Ernest Orlando Lawrence Award and is a fellow of the American Association for the Advancement of Science, the American Physical Society, and Los Alamos National Laboratory. Sarrao's research and technical leadership has emphasized national security science, from plutonium physics research to advanced materials design and discovery and stewardship of high-performance computing resources and simulation capabilities. Sarrao received his Ph.D. and master's degree in physics from the University of California, Los Angeles, and a bachelor's degree in physics from Stanford University.

Toby Smith oversees matters related to science and innovation policy, broader impacts of science, and Association of American Universities' (AAU) international activities. He shares responsibility for matters concerning research costs and other regulatory and compliance issues, including facilities and administrative costs, export controls, scientific openness and security, public access to research results, and technology transfer. He also staffs the AAU Senior Research Officers constituent group. Smith previously worked as a federal relations representative for the University of Michigan and Massachusetts Institute of Technology. He began his career as a legislative assistant to Congressman Bob Traxler (D-MI). Smith serves on the Advisory Board of the International Network for Advancing and Evaluating the Societal Impact of Science; is a member of the Council of Experts for the NSF-sponsored Center for Advancing Research Impact in Society; and is co-chair of Engaging Scientists and Engineers in Policy, an ad hoc alliance of organizations focused on helping scientists and engineers to effectively engage in the policymaking process at all levels of government. He writes and speaks widely on issues of science policy. He is the co-author of a 2008 book on national science policy titled *Beyond Sputnik – U.S. Science Policy in the 21st Century*. He is active in the American Association for the Advancement of Science, where he is honorific fellow and officer of the Societal Impacts of Science and Engineering section (Section X). He also serves as a member of the AAAS Committee on Science, Engineering and Public Policy. He holds a master's degree in legislative affairs from George Washington University and a bachelor's degree in general studies from the University of Michigan.

Patricia Valdez is a health science policy analyst at the National Institutes of Health (NIH) and serves as the extramural research integrity officer in the NIH Office of Extramural Research (OER). In this position, she serves as a liaison between the NIH and the Department of Health and Human Services' Office of Research Integrity and handles allegations of research misconduct in NIH-funded extramural activities. She has been involved in the implementation of updates to NIH grant applications and reviewed language aimed at enhancing the reproducibility of biomedical science through rigor and transparency. Valdez received her Ph.D. in molecular and cell biology from the University of California, Berkeley, and carried out her postdoctoral training in immunology discovery at Genentech. She then joined the NIH as an intramural staff scientist in the National Institute of Allergy and Infectious Diseases' Laboratory of Clinical Infectious Disease. Prior to joining OER, Valdez served as the manager of publication ethics for the American Society for Biochemistry and Molecular Biology.

Maria T. Zuber* is the E.A. Griswold Professor of Geophysics and presidential advisor for science and technology policy at Massachusetts Institute of Technology, tracking trends and seizing opportunities to inform and advance enlightened state and federal policy. She also provides strategic direction to campus labs, centers, and initiatives connected to defense or national security and represents MIT with external stakeholders. Zuber served as vice president for research from 2013 to 2024, and was responsible for research administration and policy, research relationships with the federal government, and oversight of MIT Lincoln Laboratory and more than a dozen interdisciplinary research laboratories and centers. In that role, she led the team that developed and provided oversight for MIT's Climate Action Plan. Zuber's research bridges planetary geophysics and the technology of space-based laser and radio systems. Since 1990, she has held leadership roles associated with scientific experiments or instrumentation on 10 NASA missions, most notably serving as principal investigator of the Gravity Recovery and Interior Laboratory, or GRAIL, mission. Zuber currently serves as chair of the Standing Review Board of NASA's Mars Sample Return mission. She holds a B.A. from the University of Pennsylvania and an Sc.M. and Ph.D. from Brown University. She has won numerous awards, including the MIT James R. Killian Jr. Faculty Achievement Award, the highest honor the MIT faculty bestows on one of its own. She is a member of the National Academy of Sciences and the American Philosophical Society and is a fellow of the American Academy of Arts and Sciences, the American Association for the Advancement of Science, the Geological Society, and the American Geophysical Union. In 2019, she was awarded the Gerard P. Kuiper Prize by the Division for Planetary Sciences of the

American Astronomical Society. Zuber is the first woman to lead a science department at MIT and the first to lead a NASA planetary mission. In 2013, President Obama appointed her to the National Science Board, and in 2018 she was reappointed by President Trump. She served as board chair from 2016 to 2018. In 2021, President Biden named her as co-chair of the President's Council of Advisors on Science and Technology.

Appendix F

The National Science, Technology, and Security Roundtable Co-Chairs' Paper

John C. Gannon, Richard A. Meserve, Maria T. Zuber

July 2024

This paper was presented at the Capstone Workshop and shared in advance with all attendees. It was revised after the workshop to incorporate comments and additional information from the workshop.

The opinions expressed here are those of the authors and do not necessarily represent positions of the other workshop participants; the National Science, Technology, and Security Roundtable; or the National Academies of Sciences, Engineering, and Medicine.

Section 1746(b) of the National Defense Authorization Act for Fiscal Year 2020 (NDAA 2020; P.L. 116-92)[1] directed the establishment of a National Science, Technology, and Security Roundtable (NSTSR) by the National Academies of Sciences, Engineering, and Medicine (the National Academies) to explore issues related to the illicit exploitation of the openness of U.S. fundamental research by certain foreign countries, principally China, in ways detrimental to U.S. national and economic security. The Statement of Task for the NSTSR arising from the congressional direction is set out in Box F-1.

Our basic mandate was to assess the growing foreign threat to open science and the effectiveness of the U.S. response to it. The NSTSR reached out to a wide range of stakeholders to discuss foreign threats and risks and to engage in a dialogue about risk management. Our objective was to gain understanding and share our observations, not necessarily to develop a consensus on substance or policy.

The membership of the NSTSR is made up of representatives of federal agencies and key stakeholders in the scientific enterprise, including universities, federal research laboratories, industry, and nonprofit organizations. The NSTSR held 14 meetings between November 2020 and September 2024 to explore issues related to its charge, including 9 sessions in Washington, D.C. and 5 regional meetings at the University of Maryland, Massachusetts Institute of Technology (MIT), Northwestern University, Hoover Institution at Stanford University, and Texas A&M University. The NSTSR has had extensive interactions with numerous federal agencies, including law enforcement and the Intelligence Community, and a wide range of people from the research community.

PURPOSE OF THIS REPORT

NDAA 2020 directs that the NSTSR shall issue publicly available reports concerning the matters covered in the Statement of Task. Because National Academies procedures prohibit roundtables from preparing consensus reports, the three co-chairs drafted this document to describe the course of the NSTSR's work and to convey our observations from our extensive deliberations. NSTSR members provided useful input to the draft in two review sessions at Texas A&M on January 6, 2024, and at the National Academies' Keck Center in Washington, D.C., on May 1, 2024,

---

[1] The text of the Section 1746(b) is set out in an addendum to this paper.

> **BOX F-1**
> **National Science, Technology, and Security Roundtable Statement of Task**
>
> The open exchange of scientific and technical information has long been a fundamental tenet of science and an important feature of academic and federally funded research in the United States. Recent reports of foreign governments acquiring information and materials from foreign students and faculty studying and working in U.S. institutions and from U.S. faculty engaged in collaborative research activities abroad are raising concerns that the open exchange of U.S. scientific and technical know-how may be presenting new national and economic security risks in an increasingly global and competitive environment. The National Academies of Sciences, Engineering, and Medicine will establish a National Science, Technology, and Security Roundtable to provide a neutral venue where individuals from the national intelligence and law enforcement communities can meet with representatives from industry and the academic research community to discuss current threats, benefits, and potential risks. The roundtable will (1) explore critical issues related to protecting U.S. national and economic security; (2) identify and consider security threats and risks associated with federally funded research and development; (3) identify effective approaches to communicating threats and risks; (4) share best practices for addressing and mitigating the threats and risks; and (5) examine potential near- and long-term responses by stakeholders in the research enterprise to mitigate and address the risks associated with foreign threats. Proceedings of the roundtable discussions will be produced as will an overarching summary at the end of 4 years.

and some of those suggestions have been incorporated into this document. We conclude with the view that much has been done but much more needs to be done within the research enterprise and by other government and private-sector stakeholders.

The co-chairs believe that an unrestricted, independent report from them is the best way to convey the full measure of the rich insights received from a wide range of stakeholders over the past 4 years and to address broader issues relevant to U.S. scientific research. This paper is divided into four sections: (1) "Bottom Lines," a brief snapshot of the current state of play on salient issues; (2) "The Vital Role of Open Science," an in-depth assessment of current challenges; (3) "A Roundup of the Roundtable's 4-Year Journey," a summary and analysis of the topics addressed by the roundtable; and (4) "Final Thoughts – Building an Offense," a summary of critical steps that should be pursued.

BOTTOM LINES

We found wide agreement that significant progress has been made over the past 4 years in containing the foreign threat, protecting open science, and defending both international engagement and the recruitment of foreign talent in our universities. Awareness of the serious and growing foreign threat, especially from China, has grown steadily across the research enterprise. Research agencies have hardened their defenses. Many universities, on their own or in response to explicit federal guidance, have developed strong risk management processes and structured research security programs. The Federal Bureau of Investigation (FBI) is collaborating in the development of research security programs at multiple universities and has begun to reach out to the Asian American academic community to address concerns about discrimination. And the Department of Justice appears to have softened the aggressive prosecutorial reach noted on some campuses during the period of the China Initiative (2018–2022), while, at the same time, collaborating more effectively with research entities to deal with increasing foreign interference.

This good news is mostly about commendable best practices that are making a difference but are not yet the standard across academic and research entities. These best practices, including closer collaboration between academia and law enforcement, clearly need to be pursued more broadly. In addition to more collaboration in the field, for example, we also have heard proposals for closer executive-level communication with the FBI in the form of a central academic relations office at FBI headquarters. But the NSTSR has observed that foreign interference, especially brazen intellectual property (IP) theft, has continued. We have done a lot, but clearly not enough!

International Engagement

The research community today recognizes that the United States no longer dominates research and development (R&D) across the world. International engagement is an imperative, not an option, for sustaining both the competitiveness of our research programs and the global attractiveness of our world-class universities.

We have observed, however, some obstacles to productive engagement. Significant help is needed, for example, from various federal agencies to ease confusing visa restrictions on foreign students, to facilitate legitimate foreign talent in joining the U.S. research enterprise, and to prevent harassment of our foreign-born students and faculty travelers during border interrogations. The protection and advancement of U.S. research, a core national security asset, should warrant a whole-of-government approach.

We also have observed formidable challenges within the international research community itself. The vast expansion of that community over the past 40 years, resulting in part from extensive nation-state scientific progress and information technology (IT)–driven globalization, has included many illiberal or authoritarian governments that cynically exploit openness and violate norms to their competitive advantage. China is only one of many governments that do not share our democratic values or play by agreed-upon rules. The United States and some of our democratic allies have taken note of this growing problem and have taken some initiatives to address it. But it will take a major coordinated and sustained effort to restore and reinvigorate the U.S.-inspired rules-based system of open research that brought such immense prosperity through the Cold War years and beyond—a system requiring commitment to shared values of research integrity, objectivity, openness, and reciprocity.

The China Threat

China is the most powerful adversary America has faced in more than a hundred years—with considerable military, diplomatic, political, economic, and scientific resources. The research community today generally accepts that China has developed significant capacity in scientific research and development. The NSTSR's dialogue revealed that the U.S. response to China's ascent comes up short in two important ways. First, the emphasis on the counterintelligence threat tends to eclipse the more serious threat to U.S. leadership arising from our failure to invest adequately in critical emerging technologies and in the fundamental science that underlays them. It is in science, not counterintelligence, that China threatens to outperform the United States. Second, evolving U.S. strategy on China should reflect a balance among three components: reciprocal collaboration where possible;

vigorous, well-funded economic and scientific competition where necessary; and strong military deterrence to prevent an unwanted war. A strategy to develop the necessary balance, especially in science, was not clear from our deliberations.

Engaging the Private Sector

The NSTSR's focus on universities reflects, in part, the federal government's capacity as a major funder to exercise some control over university research. In recent years, however, the private sector has played an increasing role in fundamental research both as a source of funds and as a research performer, resulting in less government involvement in such work.[2] In some fields (e.g., artificial intelligence [AI] and biotechnology) research by the private sector bears a strong connection to national and economic security, which means there should be much deeper engagement with the private sector in threat mitigation, information sharing, and protection of fundamental research from foreign interference.

Risk Management

We found strong agreement that state-of-the-art risk management is an imperative across the U.S. research enterprise, and that foreign research collaboration must be reciprocal and based on thoughtful risk-return analysis. We conclude, however, that this model of rigorous, technology-based risk assessment is still a work in progress in most research entities. A strengthened process would weigh both the threat to economic or national security arising from openness and the risk to research competitiveness and advance by constraining openness. The aim should be to structure a good-faith evaluation of legitimate interests of science and security, guided by objective data from all relevant sources. The bottom line, though still largely aspirational, is that science and security need to be together at the table from the beginning.

---

[2] Although the federal government is the largest funder of basic research (40 percent in 2021), the federal government's share of basic research funding is now only slightly larger than that funded by the business sector, which increased its support from 20 percent in 2011 to 36 percent in 2021. While universities are the most significant performer of basic research (46 percent), business performs 35 percent of such work. For further information, see https://ncses.nsf.gov/pubs/nsb20243/discovery-u-s-and-global-r-d.

THE CRITICAL ROLE OF OPEN SCIENCE

U.S. global leadership in scientific research arose at the end of World War II when the government made substantial investments to harness and build on major wartime scientific advances. In 1947, the first federally funded research and development centers (FFRDCs) were launched. These include national laboratories established by a variety of departments to pursue research related to agency missions; FFRDCs are typically operated by corporations or universities. Perhaps the most wide-reaching change arose from the issuance of *Science, The Endless Frontier*, authored by Vannevar Bush in 1945 and delivered to President Truman. It resulted in an alteration of the entire landscape for the conduct of basic research. Guided by the transformative effect of science on our wartime capabilities, it became national policy to provide significant federal support for fundamental science in universities, thereby generating a synergistic coupling of scientific advance with the training of scientists and engineers. This ultimately resulted in the creation of research universities throughout the United States and led to a flowering in scientific and technical capability. An essential element of the new paradigm was the recognition of the value of open research—a perspective repeatedly underscored by representatives of the scientific community in their interactions with the NSTSR.

Science and technology have been the critical means by which the United States has enhanced security, grown our economy, and nurtured improvements in our way of life. The new markets, industries, companies, and military capabilities that emerged from our science and technology capacity have combined to make the United States the most secure and economically prosperous nation on Earth. Remarkable changes in the way we live and work are the product of science and technology—in defense, agriculture, health care, communications, energy, and on and on.

Advances in science and technology have enabled the United States to generate more than 20 percent of global gross domestic product with only about 4 percent of the world's population.

In the twenty-first century, however, the U.S. research enterprise faces a rapidly changing world that requires much stronger efforts to safeguard the results of scientific research from foreign interference. The challenges include the following:

- China has become a peer competitor with a steadily advancing science and technology (S&T) innovation ecosystem and immense

capacity to pursue its goals to develop a world-class cadre of scientists and to lead in the discovery of path-breaking technologies.
- Other countries that have long been sources of talent at U.S. research universities have invested in science for economic gain and to keep top-achieving students at home.
- IT-driven globalization of R&D—exponentially enhanced by AI and machine learning—has intensified both the competitiveness and the interconnectedness of international research. It is arguably harder than ever to protect intellectual property.

The more complex and competitive international environment has changed perceptions of risks, threats, and opportunities and has increased concern that individuals and institutions in other countries are using illicit means to exploit research openness in ways that jeopardize U.S. security and economic competitiveness. This concern is warranted, but in some cases has produced actions that arguably sacrifice the advantages of openness in the name of increased security against perceived security threats.

We can no longer assume that the United States is and will remain uniquely preeminent in all fields of science and technology. Other countries have observed the strength that has resulted from our past investments and are seeking to emulate the path we have followed. China, in particular, has a declared national goal of becoming the world leader in certain critical fields—for example, quantum computing, artificial intelligence and machine learning, biotechnology, microelectronics, and advanced manufacturing. It is making large investments, greater in some of these areas than the United States is making. It has a well-educated and growing labor force in science and technology. China now awards more than twice as many first degrees (roughly equivalent to a bachelor's degree) in science and engineering than the United States and recently exceeded the United States in the award of Ph.D.'s. China has been the top producer in the world of Ph.D.'s in the natural sciences since 2007.[3] In some fields, China may well have obtained peer status or even attained preeminence compared with the United States. This is evidenced by the fact that the output of published

---

[3] NSB, NSF (National Science Board, National Science Foundation). *2024. Science and Engineering Indicators 2024: The State of U.S. Science and Engineering*. NSB-2024-3. Alexandria, VA. https://ncses.nsf.gov/pubs/nsb20243/talent-u-s-and-global-stem-education-and-labor-force.

articles in science and engineering by Chinese researchers is almost double the output of the United States.[4]

Based on the briefings we have received from the law enforcement and intelligence communities, it is clear that the Chinese Communist Party has engaged in illegal or duplicitous means to obtain knowledge on scientific and technical matters from research in the United States and around the world. These include extensive cybersecurity intrusions to obtain access to information and solicitation of inappropriate assistance from some U.S.-based researchers that conflict with their commitments to their U.S. employers and federal funding agencies.

One obvious possible means to respond to the threat of illicit appropriation of fundamental research is to seek to constrain access by researchers from countries of concern. The NSTSR heard near-universal recognition that such a strategy, if applied broadly, would entail risk to our own scientific capabilities. Indeed, as recognized by the NDAA 2020 itself, openness, including open interaction with the international community, is an essential characteristic of fundamental research and should be constrained only in narrow areas and/or specific projects where the risks are great. There are several reasons for this:

- Open communication is the engine that facilitates scientific progress and restricting it risks loss for all contributors.
- Foreign-born researchers in the United States are important contributors to our research enterprise and the loyalty of most to the United States is not in question. We would hobble U.S. advance if any significant part of our scientific community is discouraged from full and effective participation. The National Science Foundation (NSF) reports:

  In 2021, foreign-born workers (regardless of citizenship status) accounted for 19% of the STEM [science, technology, engineering, and mathematics] workforce. Foreign-born workers accounted for 19% of workers in S&E [science and engineering] occupations at the bachelor's degree level, 37%

---

[4] NSB, NSF (National Science Board, National Science Foundation). 2023. Publications Output: U.S. Trends and International Comparisons. *Science and Engineering Indicators 2024,* figure PBS-2. NSB-2023-33. Alexandria, VA. https://ncses.nsf.gov/pubs/nsb202333/.

Note: The analysis does not include an assessment of the comparative significance of the articles.

at the master's degree level, and 43% at the doctorate level. ... More than half of doctorate-level computer and mathematical scientists and engineers—occupations associated with critical and emerging technologies by the National Science Board (NSB 2022)—working in the United States were born outside the country. Including workers of all education levels, India and China were the leading birthplaces of foreign-born S&E workers in the United States, accounting for 29% and 12%, respectively, of all foreign-born S&E workers.[5]

- There are areas in which researchers in other countries, including China, are making pathbreaking discoveries and U.S. researchers benefit from access to their work. Indeed, global collaboration in research has become the norm, and actions that limit interaction with the global community will ultimately be counterproductive to the vitality of the U.S. research enterprise.[6] The key requirements are openness, compliance with rules, and reciprocity so that the various parties to an international collaboration fully share and benefit from the results.

In sum, openness is an essential characteristic of the fundamental research that underlies our national and economic security and should only be constrained where the risks of openness clearly exceed the benefits.

Particular concern has been expressed about the large numbers of foreign scientists and engineers who are trained at U.S. universities and who may return to countries of concern with skills that facilitate technical advance in worrisome areas. The data show that a significant portion of the foreign students who obtain Ph.D.'s or pursue postdoctoral appointments in the United States remain here as productive members of the U.S. scientific workforce. The NSF reports that the 10-year stay rate for engineering, the most common S&E doctoral field of temporary visa holders, was 72 percent. S&E doctorate recipients with Chinese citizenship at graduation had average 5-year and 10-year stay rates of 88 percent and

---

[5] NSB, NSF, *Science and Engineering Indicators 2024*. https://ncses.nsf.gov/pubs/nsb20243/talent-u-s-and-global-stem-education-and-labor-force.

[6] American Academy of Arts and Sciences. 2020. *America and the International Future of Science*, Cambridge, MA. https://www.amacad.org/publication/interntional-science.

81 percent, respectively.[7] Although concern may appropriately arise that a small percentage of the students in fact are collection agents, actions that discourage the inflow of scientific talent will weaken our long-term capability. This is particularly the case because U.S. citizens are not available in sufficient numbers to fulfill the staffing needs of the U.S. S&T enterprise. Although not in the purview of the NSTSR, it is clear that the United States should redouble its efforts to increase the pool of domestic STEM talent.

If the results of fundamental research are customarily published and available to all, one might appropriately ask why there is concern about illicit efforts to obtain that information. The reasons arise from the advantages that can accrue from some aspects of open research. For example, although scientists customarily provide details of their methodology in publications, there is often considerable "know-how" that is developed by a researcher in the conduct of the work. Luring a researcher to establish duplicative facilities in China or to train scientists abroad on laboratory skills enables the transfer of the full capability to undertake the research and even to gain insights as to productive new directions. Another example relates to applications for federal grants. Proposals to federal agencies are subject to peer review but are held confidential until grants are awarded. Early access to research proposals or perhaps even pre-publications can provide a means to determine future research directions and to jump-start research projects.

Moreover, if the foreign efforts of a U.S. researcher are concealed, federal funds may be squandered on duplicative research. This is ultimately unfair to other applicants who otherwise might legitimately obtain funding.

The United States has confronted issues arising from the openness of fundamental research before. There was warranted concern about a sustained effort by the Soviet Union to steal U.S. technology for military advantage during the Cold War. Guided by a careful review of the issues

---

[7] NSF, *The State of U.S. Science and Engineering 2024.* https://ncses.nsf.gov/pubs/nsb20243/talent-u-s-and-global-stem-education-and-labor-force.

See also J. Corrigan, J. Dunham, and R. Zwetsloot, 2022, *The Long-Term Stay Rates of International STEM PhD Graduates,* Center for Security and Emerging Technology. https://cset.georgetown.edu/publication/the-long-term-stay-rates-of-international-stem-phd-graduates/

by the National Academies,[8] the Reagan administration issued National Security Decision Directive 189 (NSDD-189),[9] which declared:

> It is the policy of this Administration that, to the maximum extent possible, the products of fundamental research remain unrestricted. It is also the policy of this Administration that, where national security requires control, that the mechanism for control of information generated during federally funded fundamental research in science, technology and engineering at colleges, universities and laboratories is classification.

The policy concluded:

> No restrictions may be placed upon the conduct or reporting of federally funded fundamental research that has not received national security classification, except as provided in applicable U.S. Statutes.

The policy was reaffirmed in 2001 and 2010. Nonetheless, it may be argued that there have been significant changes in the research enterprise that justify a different approach. The gap between research and application in some important fields has closed and, unlike times past, commercial products play an increasingly important role in national security systems. The need for protection of unclassified work has thus arguably grown.

The control of unclassified information arising from scientific research has expanded over recent years by designating it as Controlled Unclassified Information (CUI).[10] The question thus arises again as to the extent to

---

[8] Institute of Medicine, National Academy of Sciences, and National Academy of Engineering. 1982. *Scientific Communication and National Security.* Washington, DC: The National Academies Press. https://doi.org/10.17226/253.

[9] The White House. 1985. "National Policy on the Transfer of Scientific, Technical and Engineering Information." National Security Decision Directive 189 (NSDD-189), September 21, 1985.

[10] There is common agreement that some types of unclassified information should be restricted. These include trade secret and proprietary commercial or financial information, medical records providing patient identity, other information that would invade personal privacy, information relating to pre-decisional deliberations within federal agencies, and law enforcement information and legally privileged communications. The concern about CUI relates to the expansion of its scope over time to encompass the results of all manner of unclassified material without formal justification. See National Archives, *Controlled Unclassified Information: CUI Categories.* https://www.archives.gov/cui/registry/category-list.

which restrictions on dissemination of the results of fundamental research should encompass not only classified information, as provided by NSDD-189, but also should be expanded to encompass unclassified research that could negatively affect national or economic security. Some have expressed concerns that restrictions on fundamental research beyond the scope of NSDD-189 would have a serious inhibiting effect by increasing the cost of research, slowing the development of new technologies, and discouraging some individuals or institutions from engaging in research in the restricted fields. There is a concern that risk-averse officials with responsibility for federal grants and contracts have incentives to be protective and could impose needless and counterproductive limitations that will erode the benefits of openness. Moreover, the proliferation of CUI restrictions has been unevenly applied, creating particular confusion among those who pursue research supported by multiple agencies. There are thus many who disagree with the application of CUI limitations beyond those required by statute (e.g., export controls). Indeed, some departments do not believe CUI limitations are necessary because the federal government controls what it funds and can simply conduct sensitive work in a non-open environment, such as at an FFRDC.

Some others see a need for control of dissemination of fundamental research using CUI restrictions in sensitive "gray areas" that fall short of classification. That is, they believe that limiting controls on dissemination to just classification and statutorily defined constraints is insufficient. But there is general agreement that the federal government should justify the imposition of any restrictions guided, in our view, by careful risk assessment.

ROUNDUP OF THE ROUNDTABLE'S 4-YEAR JOURNEY

The following narrative describes the progress and challenges encountered by the NSTSR during its 4-year tenure. It is structured to respond to the five tasks defined in the Statement of Task and in NDAA 2020.

First Task: Explore Critical Issues Related to Protecting U.S. National and Economic Security While Ensuring the Open Exchange of Ideas

The NSTSR's membership consists of past and present senior leaders of scientific or national security entities, along with ex officio representatives from government agencies and the private sector. Among this group, there was no shared perception of the foreign threat across the research enterprise at the time of the NSTSR's first formal meeting in November 2020. The Department of Justice's China Initiative of 2018, which targeted and unsettled the research community—especially scholars of Chinese origin (including U.S. citizens)—was in full operation. Distrust between academia and law enforcement existed in varying degrees, which inhibited collaboration in many instances.

There was confusion and anxiety, especially in research universities committed to open science, about the scale and scope of foreign interference—especially from the Chinese Communist Party—and about the potentially adverse effect of stronger regulation on time-tested research practices, on essential international engagement, and on the research enterprise's reliance on foreign talent. These concerns and others were reflected in questions during a 2020 webinar sponsored by the Office of Science and Technology Policy (OSTP).[11] Many participants asked whether the alleged prevalence of security breaches involved isolated incidents or the whole research enterprise. Others expressed growing fear of racial profiling in investigations.

In our first year, the NSTSR conducted fact finding, including interaction with funding agencies, congressional staff, OSTP and the Joint Committee on the Research Environment, various universities and labs, and multiple research associations. In particular, we met with senior staff at the National Institutes of Health (NIH) and National Science Foundation to hear directly how breaches were identified and managed, and to explore the relationship with law enforcement. We also reviewed key studies focused on our issues, including the 2019 JASON study *Fundamental Research Security*, which explored the value of open science, international engagement, and foreign talent, while warning against new restrictions on fundamental research and recommending that conflicts of interest and disclosure breaches be handled within the framework of rule-based research integrity.[12]

JASON had seen some concerning evidence on Chinese Communist Party interference, but concluded that "the scale and scope of the problem remain poorly defined and academic leadership, faculty, and front-line government agencies lack a common understanding of foreign influence in U.S. fundamental research, the possible risks derived from it, and the possible detrimental effects of restrictions on it that might be enacted in

---

[11] Office of Science and Technology Policy. n.d. "OSTP Regional Webinar on Research Security: Consolidated Questions." Undated document provided to the roundtable in 2020.

[12] JASON. 2019. *Fundamental Research Security*. JSR-19-2I. https://www.nsf.gov/news/special_reports/jasonsecurity/JSR-19-2IFundamentalResearchSecurity_12062019FINAL.pdf.

response."[13] This stands in contrast to the views 4 years later of both JASON and the NSTSR regarding both the China risk and the response of academia, both of which developed a keener understanding of the risks posed by the intentions of the Chinese Communist Party.[14]

Second Task: Identify Foreign Threats and Risks

The NSTSR's grasp of the foreign threat, unclear at the start, became sharper as we interacted with academia, think tanks, and the Intelligence Community. Think tank input reinforced the description of China as a powerful U.S. peer competitor, inextricably linked economically to the United States, but openly determined to surpass our global reputation for technology innovation—and with the capacity to keep closing the gaps through licit and illicit means.

The NSTSR concluded that "threat and risk" must pertain both to the counterintelligence challenge of containing foreign interference and the growing research challenge of competing with China's formidable S&T innovation ecosystem. The NSTSR also came to recognize that the threat to U.S. scientific research comes not only from major state adversaries but also from smaller states and transnational bad actors empowered by advanced technologies in an electronically borderless world.

National Security Presidential Memorandum–33 (NSPM-33)[15] specified the obligations of various federal agencies in responding to the threat of foreign interference, issued in January 2021. But guidance as to the obligations of universities was not defined at that time, with the result that the NSTSR continued to hear concerns from university administrators, faculty, and bench scientists. Some academics forcefully argued that greater local initiatives in upholding research integrity were far preferable to more law enforcement on campuses.

---

[13] JASON, *Fundamental Research Security*, p. 2.

[14] JASON. 2024. *Safeguarding the Research Enterprise.* https://nsf-gov-resources.nsf.gov/files/JSR-23-12-Safeguarding-the-Research-Enterprise-final.pdf?VersionId=ZVhvRaTIrxMsdZql6E_yz5pN6Ssw0fSl. The 2024 report cites major global changes complicating the research landscape, including "the continuing rise of the PRC as a peer competitor to the United States, together with concerns about the PRC's policies of military-civil fusion," p. 10.

[15] The White House. 2021. "Presidential Memorandum on United States Government-Supported Research and Development National Security Policy." National Security Presidential Memorandum – 33 (NSPM-33), January 14, 2021.

Calls came for more reliable information about the specific implications of the foreign threat against universities. On October 5, 2021, NSTSR co-chair Maria Zuber in testimony to the U.S. House Committee on Science, Space, and Technology, provided a defense of open science coupled with a recommendation for more rigorous risk management of collaboration with China. She stated that the NSTSR was working with law enforcement to get "information needed to evaluate what percentage of faculty that may be engaging in improper activities, and how big of a threat they represent."[16]

The NSTSR co-chairs, in consultation with staff and responding to the oft-asked question about the precise threat posed by the Chinese Communist Party to academia, decided on a work plan that would initially concentrate on universities, where the vulnerability of open science to foreign interference seemed greater than in the private-sector research community, where protection of intellectual property was the norm.

The NSTSR's own research, backed up by Intelligence Community and academic briefings, confirmed the need for greater intelligence support for academia amidst a growing Chinese Communist Party threat, but not a high number of recorded incidents of successful Chinese intelligence operations against U.S. universities. The Washington-based think tank CSIS (Center for Strategic and International Studies), reported fewer than 10 university-related incidents among 224 cases of Chinese illicit operations since 2000.[17] Most such operations were directed against U.S. military, commercial, or political targets. This, of course, does not account for all illicit foreign intelligence activity against academia. Moreover, many of the collection efforts directed at academia are not through traditional intelligence techniques, but through nontraditional methods. According to the FBI, the number of cyber "hits" on research entities remains high, in part because the Chinese Communist Party is increasingly seeking sensitive data from research universities. Most academic targets, however, are select faculty and postdocs, not the bulk of foreign-born faculty and students in our universities.

---

[16] Zuber, M. T. 2021. Testimony to the House Committee on Science, Space, and Technology, October 5, 2021. https://www.congress.gov/117/meeting/house/114100/witnesses/HHRG-117-SY21-Wstate-ZuberM-20211005.pdf.

[17] Center for Strategic and International Studies. 2023. *Survey of Chinese Espionage in the United States Since 2000.* https://www.csis.org/programs/strategic-technologies-program/survey-chinese-espionage-united-states-2000.

APPENDIX F   129

According to the FBI assessment, *China: The Risk to Academia*:

> [Most] international scholars on US campuses pose no threat to their host institutions, fellow classmates, or research fields. ... While the vast majority of students and researchers from China are in the United States for legitimate academic reasons and contribute to the diversity of backgrounds and ideas important to our society, the Chinese government uses some Chinese students—mostly post-graduate student and post-doctorate researchers studying science, technology, engineering, and mathematics (STEM)—and professors to operate as non-traditional collectors of intellectual property.[18]

The large majority of foreign science researchers are recognized by U.S. law enforcement as integral to the U.S. research community.

The FBI engaged with the NSTSR from the outset of its work. We received initial briefings from the Director of National Intelligence (DNI) and FBI officers on July 7, 2021, which focused heavily on China. The FBI's counterintelligence chief brought a veteran team to the Keck Center on January 26, 2022, for further briefings, which improved our understanding of China's particular threat to academia. Special agents at Northwestern and Stanford Universities briefed on counterintelligence issues and the foreign threat to universities. On September 15, 2022, the Central Intelligence Agency provided detailed classified briefings at the Keck Center, including a focus on China, Russia, and the challenge of emerging technologies, from a senior team from the agency's Transnational and Technology Mission Center, the China Mission Center, the Counterintelligence Mission Center, and the Directorate of Science and Technology. It was clear that intelligence support would be helpful to the research enterprise in assessing the evolving China threat, and also in tracking the trajectory of emerging technologies as adversaries might see them.

The 2024 *Annual Threat Assessment of the U.S. Intelligence Community* focused on the familiar four principal state threats to the United States, directly or indirectly affecting U.S.-sponsored S&T research, although lesser state and nonstate risks abound in the acutely interconnected world of

---

[18] FBI (Federal Bureau of Investigation). 2019. *China: The Risk to Academia.* https://www.fbi.gov/file-repository/china-risk-to-academia-2019.pdf/view.

scientific R&D.[19] This current Intelligence Community assessment is consistent with the picture presented in the NSTSR's briefings, consultations, and discussions over the past few years.

The four states named by the DNI are China, Russia, Iran, and North Korea. China, the only U.S. peer competitor, is investing heavily in indigenous innovation, prioritizing advance power and energy, AI and machine learning, quantum information science, and semiconductors—while it aggressively acquires foreign IP partly through theft. Russia, a distant but menacing second, uses its considerable espionage and cyber capabilities as principal instruments of foreign policy. For example, it is the main suspect in the SolarWinds breach of NIH in December 2020.[20] Both Iran and North Korea are declared U.S. adversaries whose cyber operations repeatedly threaten U.S. and allied networks and data. Both countries have conducted multiple cyber operations against the United States, with North Korea launching a major attack on the U.S. movie industry in 2014.

The foreign threat assessment directly affecting the research enterprise includes many other less prominent states, international organizations, and networks that are empowered by cyber and AI capabilities, as well as by their extensive collaboration with better-connected players in the increasingly interconnected world of global R&D. Technology-empowered transnational threats are raising concerns about increasing hostile military capabilities and rising global conflict, about competition in space, about the security implications of climate change, and about the potential dual-use trajectory of emerging technologies. According to the DNI, "New technologies—particularly in the fields of AI and biotechnology—are being developed and are proliferating at a rate that makes it challenging for companies and governments to shape norms regarding civil liberties, privacy, and ethics. The convergence of these emerging technologies is likely to create breakthroughs, which could lead to the rapid development of asymmetric threats."[21]

The NSTSR's early decision to explore the case for fundamental research culminated in a 2-day workshop on openness, November 15–16, 2022, which convened six strategically focused panels to build on prelimi-

---

[19] DNI (Office of the Director of National Intelligence). 2024. *Annual Threat Assessment of the U.S. Intelligence Community,* February 5, 2024. https://www.dni.gov/files/ODNI/documents/assessments/ATA-2024-Unclassified-Report.pdf.

[20] See, for example, https://www.gao.gov/blog/solarwinds-cyberattack-demands-significant-federal-and-private-sector-response-infographic.

[21] See DNI, *Annual Threat Assessment,* p. 30, for discussion of disruptive technologies.

APPENDIX F

nary findings from four previous NSTSR meetings held over the previous 18 months. The foreign threat was a thread that ran through the sessions, but the focus, as intended, was on open science. The data-based presentations from experienced speakers from relevant disciplines made the case for

- scientific research as a core national security asset and key driver of U.S. economic competitiveness;
- the existential U.S. requirement for international engagement in open research to capture fresh ideas and stimulate innovation;
- our vital dependence on recruitment of foreign STEM talent to increase our competitiveness;
- our growing requirement for state-of-the-art risk management both to protect research and to contain foreign threats to it; and
- our continuing need for closer collaboration between the national security agencies and the scientific research community in developing rigorous risk management to counter foreign interference.

As reported in the workshop proceedings, keynote speaker Ernest Moniz, former U.S. secretary of energy and MIT professor, "noted that while the current focus on China is both appropriate and helpful, the United States should neither overestimate China's abilities nor underestimate China's determination to overtake the United States. He underscored the sustainable advantage created by the U.S. approach to scientific advancement based on openness and international collaboration, as compared to the Chinese Communist Party's renewed penchant for control."[22]

Third Task: Identify Effective Approaches to Communicating Threats and Risks

Over the course of the NSTSR's work, numerous approaches to communicating threats and risks were suggested, but their effectiveness is mixed. Communication is challenging because the culture in law enforcement is distinctively different from that in academia and because of limitations in the nature of information exchange. More success in communication has been achieved among the intelligence community and academia, owing to

---

[22] National Academies of Sciences, Engineering, and Medicine. 2023. *Openness, International Engagement, and the Federally Funded Science and Technology Research Enterprise: Proceedings of a Workshop – in Brief.* Washington, DC: The National Academies Press. https://doi.org/10.17226/27091, pp. 4-5.

their shared analytical perspective. Among academics, awareness and appreciation of the threat is greater among those with more access to information on foreign influence.

There have been numerous instances of troubling foreign interactions, often dating from times when formal guidance on reporting was nonexistent or vague. However, the reporting of university breaches has been limited to repetition of a small number of high-profile cases.

Because of limited information exchange, the most serious threats are not always conveyed. This is at least in part because law enforcement is unable to discuss investigations in progress or those with national security sensitivities. But the initial take-away of the academic community, given the paucity of information, was that there was little evidence of substantive concerns. Even after the wind-down of the China Initiative, the Asian-origin community of U.S. researchers, both international scholars and U.S. citizens, continue to believe they are subject to ethnic profiling by the U.S. government.

Numerous convenings and small-group or individual discussions have resulted in improved communication. There is a growing acceptance that federal actions are needed to increase research security, with motivations ranging from genuine appreciation for the increased threat to recognition of the necessity to comply with such actions in order to continue to do research in cutting-edge science and technology; an increasingly frequent reaction from faculty to senior research officers is, "Just tell me what I need to do." There are additional steps that would further help inform "the why." Leaders in all sectors should reaffirm the core values of the United States and the U.S. S&T system, drawing distinction between the U.S. open system and the People's Republic of China's autocratic control. As part of this, the United States should promote a fundamental cultural change in how the U.S. research community views research security issues—recognizing the threats as well as the benefits of international engagement. It is essential to reinforce the value of contributions made by foreign talent, including international students, scholars, and collaborators.

Fourth Task: Share Best Practices for Mitigating Risks

We understand "best practices" to relate principally to the achievement of closer collaboration between science and security in countering foreign interference while simultaneously preserving our deeply rooted commitment to openness in fundamental research to the extent possible. The single-best business practice, in our view, was OSTP's year-long

APPENDIX F   133

development of the NSPM-33 Implementation Guidance, which was undertaken in collaboration with research entities, funding agencies, other stakeholders, and in episodic consultation with the NSTSR. The Implementation Guidance has given administrators, faculty, and bench scientists greater understanding of new security regulations and provided practical tools for compliance.[23]

In our regional meetings at universities in the Northeast, Midwest, Pacific, and South of the country, we sought to engage with labs, the private sector, and the larger research community and to test the reaction of multiple universities to the NSPM-33 Implementation Guidance.

- On May 22, 2022, in Boston, we met with the FBI, the U.S. Attorney, and the MIT Strategy Group that produced a thoughtful report to guide MIT's actions.[24] The MIT report argues for a comprehensive approach to risk management involving new concrete initiatives from Congress, the executive branch, and the research universities—as well as much greater information sharing and collaboration across the universities—a classic whole-of-government approach. The MIT report provides a particularly strong example of a university taking responsibility for rigorous risk management. Relations with the FBI at MIT, unfortunately, were complicated by lingering ill feelings over the prolonged, eventually dropped prosecution of MIT professor Gang Chen. Interactions between MIT and the Department of Justice subsequent to the NSTSR convening have been more positive.
- At the October 11–12, 2023, Midwest Regional Meeting, the NSTSR heard from the Central Midwest Research Security

---

[23] NSTC (National Science and Technology Council). 2022. *Guidance for Implementing National Security Presidential Memorandum 33 (NSPM-33) on National Security Strategy for United States Government-Supported Research and Development*. A Report by the Subcommittee on Research Security and the Joint Committee on the Research Environment, January 2022. https://www.whitehouse.gov/wp-content/uploads/2022/01/010422-NSPM-33-Implementation-Guidance.pdf.

[24] MIT (Massachusetts Institute of Technology). 2022. *University Engagement with China: An MIT Approach*. https://global.mit.edu/wp-content/uploads/2022/11/FINALUniversity-Engagement-with-China_An-MIT-Approach-Nov2022.pdf.

Note: Roundtable Co-Chair Zuber of MIT recused herself from the development of the MIT China report. As a current co-chair of the President's Council of Advisors on Science and Technology, she sought to avoid any potential conflict between report recommendations and Biden administration policy on China.

Forum (University of Cincinnati, Purdue University, University of Michigan, Northwestern University) and from vice presidents of research (Georgia Tech, Michigan, University of Illinois Urbana-Champaign, and Notre Dame University). In contrast to the sentiments expressed in the Northeastern meeting, academic participants rendered enthusiastic reports about excellent relations with the FBI and progress with NSPM-33-mandated compliance.

- On March 6–7, 2024, at our Southern Regional Meeting at Texas A&M, we heard highly positive reports on FBI collaboration from representatives of Texas A&M, Tulane University, Alabama A&M, and Prairie View A&M. The FBI was described as not just accessible but proactively helpful in providing information and advice about security issues.

The NSTSR's good-news account of science-security collaboration captures data from only a small percentage of U.S. research entities, but it is enough to show an encouraging improvement in collaboration between academia and law enforcement.

Fifth Task: Assess the Foreign Threat Responses of Research-Enterprise Stakeholders

Today the full research community, including academia, has a more sophisticated grasp of the threats and risks, especially from the People's Republic of China. The restricted research community in government and industry have hardened their defenses, and universities, labs, and funding agencies all have responded to NSPM-33's welcome Implementation Guidance. The termination of the China Initiative in February 2022 has demonstrably lessened, but did not fully expunge, the chill felt by ethnic Chinese and other Asian and Asian American students and faculty. The NSTSR's meetings suggest that, while progress has been made, more needs to be done to reassure this community. Press reports continue to reveal discouraging problems that Chinese students are having with U.S. visa policies and with clearing immigration at U.S. airports, even when in possession of valid visas.[25]

---

[25] Kuo, L., and C. Cadell. 2024. "Chinese Students, Academics Say They're Facing Extra Scrutiny Entering U.S." *The Washington Post,* March 14, 2024. https://www.washingtonpost.com/world/2024/03/14/china-united-states-university-studentsborder/.

Within research organizations, stakeholders have implemented a variety of steps to mitigate and address risks associated with foreign threats. The most active and best-resourced research organizations are most cognizant of risks and have done the most to address the problem. Less-resourced organizations, including R-02 research facilities and smaller universities and colleges, do not have the resources to invest in enhancing research security and risk being shut out of the educational and entrepreneurial benefits associated with participation in the vibrant U.S. open research enterprise.

Near-Term Responses

In the short term, the implementation of NSPM-33 is mitigating inadvertent noncompliance. Actions such as standardization of forms across agencies, the use of digital CVs, reporting of all sources of funding (not limited to federal grants), and reporting international collaborations whether there is funding involved or not, lead to transparency about research support and should make it more straightforward for institutions and individuals to comply. The Implementation Guidance also calls for universities with a substantial research base to develop research security plans that include training, enhanced export control support and increased cyber controls. The establishment of NSF's SECURE (Safeguarding the Entire Community in the U.S. Research Ecosystem) Center is an example of a resource to help the community understand and navigate research security risks. Even with NSPM-33's much-appreciated standardization, new compliance requirements continue to make U.S. researchers less efficient. As discussed previously, the CUI designation is a particular burden and should be revisited by the U.S. government with the objective of limiting its scope, achieving consistency in application, and providing clear guidance on how to handle such information. Authority to designate CUI should require training and a relatively high level of authority and not be within the purview of a program manager.

Long-Term Responses

Federal agencies have been considering a variety of means to enhance security surrounding sensitive research topics. The Department of Energy, for example, has pursued a focus on the identification of critical technologies. The Department of Defense has alternatively developed a plan for certain high-risk researchers to potentially face exclusion from working on certain federal grants. A second report by JASON recommended a project-specific approach to assessing research security risk that considers Technology Readiness Level, or TRL, where appropriate.[26]

Research security vulnerabilities in industry merit scrutiny, particularly foreign investments in start-ups. Although universities may be a party to licenses that derive from research on their campuses, they have neither transparency into nor authority regarding investors in subsequent start-ups. There may be an expanded role for the interagency Committee on Foreign Investment in the United States.

According to NSTSR discussions, federal agencies should monitor which actions appear to be most effective in reducing the risk of foreign influences, while preserving openness to the extent possible. Agencies should also share best practices. In addition, the government should consult with international partners with similar cultures and norms as the United States who are experiencing similar challenges. Given the global nature of research, international cooperation is necessary; a research program is only as secure as the security level of its least secure collaborator.

In the view of many speakers at NSTSR sessions, if all we do is impose costly and time-consuming restrictions on U.S. researchers while adversaries are increasing their investments in research, the United States will not maintain preeminence. The passage of the bipartisan CHIPS and Science Act (P.L. 117-167) represents important recognition of this reality. However, unfortunately the "Science" part of the bill was authorized but not appropriated. And the FY 2024 budget was generally devastating for science agencies despite broad recognition of the importance of science investment to maintain security and economic competitiveness. Investment in science that includes attraction and training of an enhanced domestic talent pool will represent a critical component of the longer-term strategy.

FINAL THOUGHTS – BUILDING AN OFFENSE

Defense clearly is not enough! Bolstering counterintelligence, by itself, will not guarantee the protection of U.S. research integrity and competitiveness. The NSTSR experience makes clear that a far more comprehensive effort is required to outpace China's maturing S&T ecosystem. The research

---

[26] JASON. 2024. *Safeguarding the Research Enterprise.* https://nsf-gov-resources.nsf.gov/files/JSR-23-12-Safeguarding-the-Research-Enterprise-Final.pdf?VersionId=ZVhvRaTIrxMsdZql6E_yz5pN6Ssw0fSl.

community's commendable efforts thus far must be aligned with a much broader and deeper whole-of-government strategy, as recommended by the FBI, MIT's *University Engagement with China* study, the recent JASON report, the congressionally directed Cyberspace Solarium Commission report of 2020, and the National Security Commission on Artificial Intelligence in 2021.[27]

The FBI's public statements support this broader approach:

> As foreign adversaries use increasingly sophisticated and creative methodologies to exploit America's free and open education environment, the United States faces an ever-greater challenge to strike a sustainable balance between unrestricted sharing and sufficient security within this education ecosystem. Through a whole-of-society approach that includes increased public awareness, academic vigilance, industry self-protection, government and law enforcement collaboration, and legislative support, the U.S. higher education system can continue to enjoy the manifold contributions that international academics provide, while minimizing the risk they (and their affiliated home governments) pose to U.S. security priorities. The FBI maintains that striking this balance is possible and necessary.[28]

Based on observations made by outside experts and members of the NSTSR over the past 4 years, this much broader, integrated effort would include the following:

- Working with allies to restore and strengthen the international U.S.-inspired rules-and-compliance-based open-research system.
- Increasing U.S. investment in cutting-edge science and innovative technologies—the key to a U.S. strategy to maintain and strengthen our S&T enterprise.
- Developing serious and sustained efforts to restructure U.S. government research contracting and business practices through consultation among government officials, research administrators, and bench scientists so as to achieve greater efficiency and

---

[27] See Cyberspace Solarium Commission, htps://www.solarium.gov/report, and National Security Commission on Artificial Intelligence, https://reports.nscai.gov/final-report/.

[28] FBI, *Risk to Academia*, p. 1.

effectiveness. The development of the Implementation Guidance for NSPM-33 should be a model.
- Increasing university liaison with the FBI by establishing a well-resourced executive-level office for academic relations with leadership committed to improved communication and collaboration.
- Starting science-security collaboration at the start of policy formulation. When the national security community concludes that elevated threats require stronger security policies relating to science and technology, working scientists and university administrators should be involved in policy formulation to identify effective solutions and, at the same time, to push back against measures likely to damage the U.S. research enterprise.
- Engaging much deeper with the private sector. Given the private sector's growing role as a funder and performer of research in critical fields, the engagement with the private sector should encompass threat mitigation, information sharing, and, where appropriate, protection of fundamental research.
- Reconsidering the controversial CUI marking, now useful to some, but confusing to many others, and disruptive to open science. The federal government should justify CUI restrictions, guided by careful risk assessment. If CUI restrictions are to be imposed, they should be in limited technical areas in which the threat to national or economic security is substantial and the risks from openness can be convincingly shown to exceed the benefits. At the least, the CUI designation should be revisited by the government with the objective of limiting its scope, achieving consistency in application, and providing clear guidance as to how to handle such information. In cases where restrictions are imposed, open research should be allowed to proceed if the researcher and the funding agency reach agreement on measures to mitigate risk, such as agreement to restrict dissemination of information relating to limited aspects of the work. A study of the usage of the CUI marking is warranted.
- Removal of visa impediments and other immigration obstacles to legitimate and value-added foreign participation in our research activities. It is in the United States' interest to recruit foreign STEM talent and to welcome continued involvement in our S&T enterprise. This does not lessen the necessity of expanding the pool of domestic STEM talent.

- Stronger efforts by both government officials and universities to reassure foreign-born researchers that their contributions to the U.S. scientific enterprise are welcome and valued. The U.S. government also should respond forcefully to continuing reports of discrimination and alleged border harassment of traveling foreign students and faculty from our universities.
- Promotion of science at all levels of the U.S. education system and society to produce increased numbers of young scientists and engineers ready and eager to excel in U.S. scientific and technical advance.

These suggestions, drawn from the 4-year NSTSR dialogue, would bolster a needed enhancement of a U.S. research enterprise essential to our national and economic security.

ADDENDUM
NATIONAL DEFENSE AUTHORIZATION ACT FOR FISCAL YEAR 2020
PUBLIC LAW 116-92
SEC. 1746. SECURING AMERICAN SCIENCE AND TECHNOLOGY

(b) National Academies Science, Technology and Security Roundtable.—

(1) IN GENERAL.—The National Science Foundation, the Department of Energy, and the Department of Defense, and any other agencies as determined by the Director of the Office of Science and Technology Policy, shall enter into a joint agreement with the Academies to create a new "National Science, Technology, and Security Roundtable" (hereinafter in this subsection referred to as the "roundtable").

(2) PARTICIPANTS.—The roundtable shall include senior representatives and practitioners from 4 Federal science, intelligence, and national security agencies, law enforcement, as well as key stakeholders in the United States scientific enterprise including institutions of higher education, Federal research laboratories, industry, and non-profit research organizations.

(3) PURPOSE.—The purpose of the roundtable is to facilitate among participants—

(A) exploration of critical issues related to protecting United States national and economic security while ensuring the open exchange of ideas and international talent required for scientific progress and American leadership in science and technology;

(B) identification and consideration of security threats and risks involving federally funded research and development, including foreign interference, cyber attacks, theft, or espionage;

(C) identification of effective approaches for communicating the threats and risks identified in subparagraph (b) to the academic and scientific community, including through the sharing of unclassified data and relevant case studies;

(D) sharing of best practices for addressing and mitigating the threats and risks identified in subparagraph (B); and

(E) examination of potential near- and long-term responses by the Government and the academic and scientific community to mitigate and address the risks associated with foreign threats.

(4) REPORT AND BRIEFING.—The joint agreement under paragraph (1) shall specify that—

(A) the roundtable shall periodically organize workshops and issue publicly available reports on the topics described in paragraph (3) and the activities of the roundtable;

(B) not later than March 1, 2020, the Academies shall provide a briefing to the relevant committees on the progress and activities of the roundtable; and

(C) the Academies shall issue a final report on its activities to the relevant committees before the end of fiscal year 2024.

(5) TERMINATION.—The roundtable shall terminate on September 30, 2024.